here's
HELP!

here's
HELP!

From the pages of
THE NATIONAL OBSERVER

Edited by **Walter Damtoft**

Dow Jones Books
Princeton, New Jersey

Introduction

Inflation. Shortages. Retirement. Jobs. Health. Safety. Education. Recreation. Hobbies. Spending. Saving. Investing.

You need help—facts, figures, suggestions, up-to-date information—to deal with the myriad problems in the marketplace and to just plain cope with modern living.

This is what HELP is all about. You cannot afford *not* to bother.

HELP is a compendium of useful, illuminating information on a vast array of subjects ranging from allergies and insomnia to college costs and the price of tennis rackets. It tells about fun things, and about frauds. It explores some current problems, and explodes myths about others. It's packed tight with good reading and common sensible advice.

What should you do *now*, for example, to avert disaster if a fire starts in your home? How can you *profit* from trash? How can you *save* on telephone toll charges? On college costs? On housing, on auto repairs? What are prudent investments? What should you know *before* considering vasectomy, or taking dancing lessons? What may be the *most surprising*, and real, handicap in seeking a job these days?

The people who sought out and found answers to questions like these, and many others, are the reporters and editors of The National Observer, the weekly publication of Dow Jones & Co., Inc. Probing, pushing, and researching with imagination and flair, they have won innumerable accolades and awards for their reports on consumer affairs. Their best, timeliest material is collected here.

Walter A. Damtoft, Senior Editor of the Observer in charge of consumer news, compiled the material for HELP. Contributors include staffers Patricia Fanning, Paul Hood, Barbara Katz, Daniel Henninger, Patrick Young, August Gribbin, John Peterson, Michael Putney, and Edwin Roberts.

This is HELP, to save you time, money, headaches—and to fight off dragons, real and imagined.

—*The Editors*

Table of Contents

Section I On Stretching Dollars

1. Coping With College Costs 1
2. Money in Trash 6
3. Clipping Costs With Coupons 9
4. Saving on Telephone Tolls 12
5. More Meat, More Soy Protein 15
6. Fighting Increases in Utility Bills 18

Section II On Keeping Safe and Healthy

1. Escaping a Home Fire 24
2. Dangers in Mobile Homes 30
3. Are Aerosols Safe Enough? 36
4. Relax and Live Longer 41
5. Spotting Injury-Causing Hazards 50
6. Warning on Gasoline 54
7. Mysteries of Allergies 56
8. Vasectomies May Cause Problems 64
9. Checking Up on Physicians 69
10. Are Useful Drugs Banned? 79
11. Seeking a Good Night's Sleep 87

Section III On Avoiding the Pitfalls

1. Truth-in-Packaging Furniture 100
2. Spotting Turquoise Substitutes 102
3. Dealing With 'Psychic' Surgery 105

4. Wrong Numbers on Yellow Pages 113
5. The Dancing School Whirl (katz)........................121
6. Keeping Veterans' Records 128
7. Look Before You Bite 130
8. Making the BBB Work 132

Section IV On Working for a Living
1. Job-Hunting Problem: Overqualification 138
2. Changing Jobs in Mid-Life 146

Section V On House and Home

1. The Condominium Crunch...152
2. Solar Heating and Cooling 158
3. Energy-Saving Homes 164
4. Tools for Home Handymen 168

Section VI On Your Automobile

1. Keeping Checked Out...172
2. The Octane Mystery 174
3. Car Costs 176
4. Check That Deadly Auto Exhaust............................178
5. Auto-Repair Complaint Centers 180

Section VII On Your Consuming Interests

1. Knitting With Machines 184
2. Knowing the Tennis Racket 189
3. Cut-Rate Encyclopedias 195
4. Buying Antiques 197
5. Little Old Winemaker You 205
6. Motorcycling Saving and Pitfalls 209
7. Family Coats of Arms 213

8. Slow Cookers 217
9. Aluminum Keys 219
10. Buying Batteries 221
11. Smell Selling.. 227
12. Meet the Metric System 232

Section VIII On Travel and Transport

1. 'Shots' for Travel 238
2. Pet-Travel Hazards.. 240
3. How to Car Pool.. 244

Coping With College Costs

 $\mathbf{B}$ ILLS for students entering college keep growing harder to meet.

Average increases in annual tuition in 1974 and other essential expenses will range from 6.4 per cent for resident students at public, two-year colleges to a dramatic 27.3 per cent for commuting students attending private, two-year colleges. Other average increases announced by the College Entrance Examination Board indicate resident students will pay 7 per cent more at public, four-year schools and 9.4 per cent more at similar private institutions. Some costs are 80 per cent above their 1970-71 levels.

Indeed, higher education has grown so costly that a West Coast educator suggests that families should take a hard look at whether they regard college as really worth the investment. And officials of the college entrance board suggest that many parents and students will have to plan much more carefully to meet the bigger bills.

For example, total costs during the 1974-75 academic year are expected to average $2,400 for a student living on campus at a public, four-year college, and $4,039 for a resident student at a private, four-year college.

The cost increases are intensifying financial pressures on middle-income families, whose college-age members usually can't qualify for scholarships and grants; most such aid is allocated to students from low-income families. To cope with the pinch, middle-income families should study educational cost data and know the available options.

1

Coping With College Costs

Some of the facts:

● Two-year institutions no longer cost much less annually than four-year institutions.

● There's no longer a great difference in expenses for students who commute and those who live on campus. For example, costs such as transportation and food have risen 100 per cent since 1970-71 for commuters to private, four-year colleges while resident-student expenses rose 26.9 per cent.

● Private four-year colleges and universities remain the most costly, but the percentage increase in tuition and fees at these institutions has been less than at other types of institutions.

● The College Board estimates these average 1974-75 educational costs for several categories: public two-year colleges, $2,153 for those living on campus, $1,922 for commuters; private two-year, $3,617, $3,287; public four-year, $2,400, $2,085; private four-year, $4,039, $3,683; proprietary, $3,817, $3,414. The budgets include tuition and fees, room and board, transportation, and personal expenses.

Before beginning to grapple with your budget, one educator recommends, you should seriously consider the option of no college.

"I do believe that many good things can come of education, but I don't think a formal education is all that's essential," says Lewis B. Mayhew, professor of higher education at Stanford University in Palo Alto, Calif. He notes that a prestige university may cost a student and his family $10,000 a year if one assumes the student would have earned about $5,000 had he gone to work. "Both parents and student should ask if this is truly the best way to invest $40,000," says Mayhew. And he says colleges have an estimated one million reluctant attenders.

If you elect college, experts advise that you plan ahead and apply early for financial aid. Consult high-school guidance counselors on the mechanics of submitting computer-ready forms, which are required to show your need. These forms are widely used in awarding student aid from government, institutional, and private scholarship funds.

To get an idea of what you may be expected to pay, consider the hypothetical family described in "Meeting College Costs," a guide available from the College Entrance Examination Board. Mary, the oldest of three children, is ready for college. Both parents work, taking home $12,515 a year. After considering provisions for eventual retirement by the 52-year-old father, and a $12,600 equity in the home, the guide says the family should expect to pay $1,353 a year toward Mary's annual higher-education bill.

Mary would probably be able to obtain enough financial aid—through a loan, scholarship, grant, or part-time work—to meet the difference in the cost of the college she chooses. Chances are good if it's a public institution, such as the University of Nebraska, where costs come to some $2,400. But there's a big gap between tuition and expenses at a private institution like Harvard, which costs about $5,850, and the $1,353 that the family expected to manage.

Mary shouldn't reject a high-cost college before even trying for aid, warns Richard Tombaugh, executive director of the National Association of Student Financial Aid Administrators. The more expensive institutions generally have more aid money, he says.

Here are some sources that students can tap to supplement their budgets:

Federal aid. Mary can apply for a bank loan of up

3

to $2,500 a year under the Guaranteed Student Loan Program. If she can find a lender agreeable to the maximum permissible 7 per cent interest, she can borrow up to $7,500 as an undergraduate, up to $10,000 to complete graduate studies, and take 10 years to repay. Congress is expected to lower the loan amount to $2,000 a year and to eliminate need tests for families with incomes of $15,000 or less.

A new program, Basic Opportunity Grants, will be expanded in 1975 to cover sophomores as well as freshmen. A million students are expected to get grants that will average $450 but which may reach a maximum of $800. However, eligibility is limited to families who can afford to pay no more than $1,150, so Mary couldn't get such a grant.

A work-study program provides about 560,000 students with part-time jobs of up to 40 hours a week at the Federal minimum wage. Colleges administer the program, as they do two other Government funds for loans and grants.

✔ Scholarships worth $375 million are distributed by 24 states.

✔ Military scholarships. Reserve Officer Training Corps (ROTC) programs have been reinstituted at many colleges that ousted them during the protests of the late 1960s. Both men and women can get Army, Navy, or Air Force scholarships which pay tuition, fees and books, plus $100 a month. The *quid pro quo* is four years of active duty and two years of reserve duty after graduation. Participation in several hours of ROTC classes a week and summer-camp attendance are other requirements. Some 19,000 students hold military scholarships; only a small percentage are women.

✔ Veterans' benefits. There's no combat requirement

to get $220 a month, plus additional money for dependents under the GI Bill.

✔ Co-op programs. Many educators say the work ethic is on the up-swing—along with prices—on college campuses. An increasingly popular, formal way to work your way through college is to take at least five years to get a degree, alternating semesters on the job with semesters on the campus.

Roy L. Wooldridge, executive director of the National Council for Co-operative Education, says the number of colleges offering co-op programs has grown from only 50 a decade ago to more than 575. Programs have broadened to take in many more disciplines besides the original engineering majors. Northeastern University in Boston is a co-op institution, with nearly all of its 15,000 students assigned to jobs. They earn an average salary of $3,016 for 26 weeks of work.

A list of colleges that offer co-op programs is available free from the National Commission for Co-operative Education, 360 Huntington Ave., Boston 12115.

Copies of "Student Expenses at Post-secondary Institutions, 1974-75," is available at guidance offices or for $2.50 from Publications Order Office, College Entrance Examination Board, Box 592, Princeton, N.J. 08540. The report has costs for more than 2,200 colleges.

Money In Trash

INFLATION has had the biggest effect on which of the following: Your refrigerator? Your garage? Your trash can?

It's the trash can, or, more precisely, its contents. Food in your refrigerator has gone up about 22 per cent in price over the past year. The automobile in the garage has gone up in list price, but that has been tempered by discounting of some models. But the value of some of the contents of trash cans has as much as tripled.

Item: Newspapers are printed on paper that costs about 15 per cent more than it cost last year. Yet when one tosses a newspaper away, its value as wastepaper is roughly three times that of a year ago.

Discarded newspapers are the gilt-edged items in the trash. But prices for some grades of scrap iron and steel match the paper increase. And there is a good market for glass bottles, and tin and aluminum cans.

The value of our cast-off materials is at record levels. Recycling, once the idealistic dream of ecologists, is becoming profitable. Environmental concerns still play a part, but conversion of used materials has become primarily a matter of cash and convenience.

True, the amount of cash involved for the individual household is small. But on a neighborhood or community scale, throwaway items assume a definite cash importance. Civic clubs, Scout troops, and churches are finding the new values of trash more easily convertible into band uniforms, summer-camp funds, and bank accounts.

Montgomery County, Maryland, is setting up a government-operated recycling system, taking over chores previously handled by volunteer groups. If it pans out as expected, it will reduce county dump problems and produce a new source of revenue.

A net profit of more than $700 a week is contemplated by the county by operating collection centers for a wide range of items, from newspapers to tin cans. Jack Dunn, director of the project, anticipates handling 231 tons of salvageable refuse a week, which at today's prices should bring $2,400 from sales to recyclers.

This is just the opening wedge. If the county program meets its goals of collecting 8 per cent of the home refuse at the community centers at a net cost of no more than landfill costs ($5 a ton), it will open the way for an even more ambitious plan. This involves building a recycling plant where not only salable goods would be recovered, but the rest of the garbage and trash would be shredded and processed into industrial fuel.

Some 40 cities around the country are in varying stages of putting to use the trash they used to throw away. Nashville, Tenn., for example, has set up a nonprofit corporation to build a trash-burning power plant to heat and air condition downtown buildings. A St. Louis public utility already is testing use of the city's throwaway material to fire its boilers. Odessa, Texas, is building a plant to recapture usable materials and shred the rest, with the idea of tilling processed refuse into nearby lands to increase their moisture retention.

The demand for waste materials apparently peaked early in 1974, but prices later in the year were far above normal. Old newspapers that sold for $18 a ton a year ago were bringing up to $55 a ton. Office wastepaper was bringing about $30 a ton in the Washington, D.C., area.

Some grades of scrap iron that sold for $50 a ton in 1973 are worth $160 a ton in 1974. Copper scrap about doubled. And even such common items as aluminum cans were going for 12 cents a pound, glass bottles for $20 a ton, and tin cans for $20 a ton.

Shortages, and fear of shortages, in many fields have contributed to the interest in scrap.

Clipping Costs With Coupons

"CLIP us for a quarter." "Let us give you a hand on the price." "Save 10 cents." "Refund." "Get one free!" Such messages on grocery coupons become especially appealing as food prices soar.

Nearly every type of food product can be yours for a few cents less if you systematically redeem manufacturers' coupons. You'll find them printed regularly on the food pages of newspapers and magazines. They also appear on food packaging and sometimes are included with the package contents.

Typically a checkout clerk at a supermarket will give you the face amount of a coupon in cash if you have purchased the item required by the coupon. Sometimes a coupon must be mailed to a manufacturer, usually with several box tops or other evidence of product purchase, for cash refunds of as much as $2. An avid coupon and box-top saver can pick up $3 to $5 a month from mailed refunds.

Mrs. Sue Allen, a Greenbelt, Md., widow, says she saved $40 in 6 months by redeeming coupons while buying groceries for her family of three. "Just last week I put the money in the bank. Right now it's in my retirement fund, but I'll have it for something special if I want it," she says. To keep track of how much she could save Mrs. Allen filled a sugar bowl with the coins she obtained for her coupons.

Mrs. Allen emphasizes she doesn't purchase unnecessary groceries in order to use all her coupons. She says she never redeems shampoo or tooth-paste coupons because she buys such items on special at a discount store. She continues to buy many products sold under supermarkets' private labels, which often are cheaper than brand-name products with coupon rebates.

"Sometimes I try a new product because I have an introductory coupon," Mrs. Allen admits. "But I probably would try it out anyway, and with a coupon I don't feel like I'm splurging quite as much."

Obviously you won't cut down your food bill if coupon clipping induces you to buy expensive frozen pastry when you normally would settle for pudding. However, alert collectors can find coupons for staples like flour, sugar, bread, and meat. Cereal is another good coupon item. And if you regularly buy snacks, convenience foods, or brand-name vegetables, there's a coupon for almost every variety.

To save the most money, make coupon clipping an organized project. Don't keep your collection of cut-outs in disarray or you'll waste valuable time and diminish your savings by overlooking coupons. What's more, fellow shoppers may become tempted to run you down with their grocery carts if you stand in a crowded supermarket line fumbling through a handful of tattered coupons.

Some tips on efficient coupon clipping:

✔ Clip newspaper food pages the day of publication. If a particular issue has coupons for many items you want, it may be worth-while to buy additional copies to get more coupons.

✔ If the product isn't pictured on the coupon, clip part of the ad if it shows a picture that may help you quickly locate the item.

✔ In the store watch for special refund displays and packages with coupons inside. If a manufacturer is temporarily promoting an item you regularly use, buy more than one package.

✔ Sort coupons and paper-clip items in categories such as dairy products, soap, paper goods, and pet foods. Make index tabs to clip to each bundle and store them in a recipe file or small box.

✔ Check for time limits on redemption and put dated coupons in a separate category. Place in order of expiration date and make an effort to spend them before undated coupons.

✔ Group coupons for the same product with the largest redemption value on top. Redeem a coupon for 20 cents off before one for 5 cents off.

✔ If you can't find a product, talk to the manager or check other supermarkets.

✔ Promptly return unused coupons to your file after shopping to avoid losing or damaging them.

✔ Don't hold undated coupons indefinitely; the product may be discontinued.

✔ Trade coupons for items you don't use to friends who do.

✔ Save labels and proof-of-purchase marks on packages to send in when manufacturers offer refunds.

Saving On Telephone Tolls

THE American Telephone and Telegraph Co. has put into effect several general rate increases for interstate long-distance calls in recent years. The increases make familiarity with details of long-distance rates more important to the cost conscious.

The easiest way to save money is by dialing calls yourself. The less assistance callers need, the fewer operators the telephone company must hire. So, in a sense, it rewards do-it-yourself callers with substantial discounts. Thus, person-to-person calls, in which the operator places the call to a specific person, are the most expensive; operator-assisted station-to-station calls, in which the operator places the call but the customer talks to anyone who answers, are cheaper. And least expensive are the customer-dialed station-to-station calls—the telephone company calls this "direct distance dialing"—not involving an operator.

A three-minute customer-dialed station-to-station call from New York to San Francisco during weekday business hours cost $1.45 in 1974. The same call placed through an operator cost $1.85. And a person-to-person call cost $3.55.

An official of the telephone company's Long Distance Division, notes that many customers believe they can save money by calling person-to-person, on the theory that there's a high risk the party called might not be available. "This is simply not so," he says. "More than half of all person-to-person calls are completed on the first attempt.

And anyway, you can miss your calling party twice and still come out ahead."

Other ways to lower bills:

● Take advantage of lower rates during nonbusiness hours. Rates are lowest on week ends (until 5 p.m. Sunday) and after 11 p.m. daily. Next cheapest are week-night calls from 5 p.m. to 11 p.m.

● If you have a short message, take advantage of special rates for station-to-station, customer-dialed calls lasting one minute, between 11 p.m. and 8 a.m.

● Schedule calls in advance where possible. If you're calling family members, for example, try to make sure that all those you want to talk to will be in when you call. If you call someone frequently, set a regular time. Avoid repeating conversation by having family members listen in on extension phones.

● Before you place a call, list the things you want to discuss.

● Keep an egg timer or wristwatch near the phone to help keep calls short.

● When calling an out-of-town business, check the directory to see if it has a toll-free "800" number or dial 800-555-1212 at no cost for information. Many businesses provide free telephone service for out-of-town customers. Local chain hotels or motels often will make reservations at units of the same chain located elsewhere.

● If you reach a wrong number, tell the operator immediately so that the charge can be taken off your bill. It helps if you know the wrong number you reached. If you get disconnected or have a poor connection, tell the operator who will reconnect you at no charge.

● If your direct-dialed call fails to go through after several attempts, ask the operator for assistance but emphasize that you want the direct-dial rate; you should be billed at the lower rate. James Lewis, in *The Consumer's Fight-Back Book* (Award Books, 235 E. 45th St., New York City 10017; 154 pages; 95 cents), suggests that any time you have trouble on a call, ask for the identifying number of the operator who assists you. If your bill is wrong, notify the telephone company.

Another suggestion from Lewis: Keep postcards by the phone. If the call isn't absolutely necessary, send a postcard.

More Meat, More Soy Protein

A money saver at many supermarkets is a blend of ground beef and textured soy protein, which usually costs from 10 to 20 cents less per pound than regular ground beef.

Many stores have also begun to sell packages of soy protein that you can mix with meat yourself, usually at even greater savings. A few supermarket chains sell the soybean product under their own brand names. At least 12 manufacturers have put out products for test marketing in some 80 metropolitan areas.

The most widely available products are: preseasoned protein distributed by Williams Foods, Webb City, Mo.; Plus Meat, by J. H. Filbert, Inc., Baltimore; and Burger Bonus, by A. E. Staley Manufacturing Co., Oak Brook, Ill.

You may have to search the shelves for the mix-your-own variety, but you can generally expect to find plenty of the ready-mixed blend if your supermarket stocks it. After its introduction in 1973, the U.S. Department of Agriculture found that the blend accounted for 26 per cent of ground-beef sales in nearly 1,500 stores owned by three major chains. Sales went up along with the price differential between the blend and regular ground beef.

So the price appeals. But what about taste and nutrition?

Textured soy protein, sometimes called textured vegetable protein, has very little taste of its own. When you mix it with meat, it absorbs meat juices and flavor. Given proper proportions of soy and meat, an extended hamburg-

15

er tastes so much like its all-meat counterpart that you probably couldn't tell unless you were simultaneously munching on an all-meat burger.

The extended meat doesn't look unusual either. Soy in the supermarket blends usually takes on the color of the meat, and the mix-it-yourself products are caramel colored.

There is some difference in texture. Soy-extended meat is chewier, drier, and more cohesive than regular ground beef. Patties hold together better, which could be a big boon when you're trying to keep hamburger from crumbling through the grills of a charcoal broiler.

There's less shrinkage too. The particles of soy retain meat juices better than meat itself does, so a cook gets double duty from the extender. You have more raw material to start with, and you lose less of it in cooking.

Soy-extended meat is also lower in fat, and therefore in both calories and cholesterol, than regular ground beef. Tests have shown that even though the soy absorbs some of the meat fat, a broiled soy burger has significantly less fat than an ordinary burger. That's because negligible fat, even of the vegetable variety, is left after processing the textured soy.

For calorie counters, here are some figures compiled by Williams Foods: a three-ounce portion of regular ground beef has 245 calories; lean ground beef has 185 calories; and blend of 30 per cent soy extender and 70 per cent regular ground beef has 162 calories. The 30 per cent soy mixture is generally accepted as the maximum that may be used without losing palatability or, more important, nutritional value. Many blends and instructions for home mixing use a 25 per cent or less soy figure.

The addition of an extender and water generally results in a soy-meat blend weighing half again as much as the meat component. A heavily seasoned extender, such as the Williams product, can be used in sufficient volume to make the blend weigh about twice its meat component.

Textured soy protein is high in nutrition. "It's so much better than the cracker crumbs, bread crumbs, and oatmeal that have been used for years to extend meat," says William W. Gallimore of the U.S. Department of Agriculture. Soy does lack some of the amino acids that are necessary to trigger the body's use of other amino acids. However, meat used in blends contains enough triggering aminos to make up for the extender's shortage, provided the maximum recommended proportion of extender isn't exceeded. So, in practical terms, extended hamburger is just about the nutritional equivalent of unblended meat.

For those who do try a soy extender with their ground beef, Williams home economist Alice Johnson has some cooking tips:

If you mix the ingredient yourself, carefully follow package directions. For example, the dried soy granules must be soaked in the proper amount of water for best results. Don't brown a blend too much because soy burns more readily than meat. Though charring sometimes enhances the flavor of meat, it won't help the soy. Cooking the mixture too long may also result in some flavor loss. Try adding about a teaspoon of sugar to improve the flavor of the finished product. And feel free to freeze either a blend or mix-it-yourself leftovers.

Gallimore warns that soy protein granules will become rancid if exposed to air during long storage, so quickly use up an opened package.

Fighting Increases in Utility Bills

Cut out the lights. Turn down the furnace. Quit phoning out-of-town relatives.

In most states that's about all a consumer can do to avoid a bigger bill if the electric, gas, or phone company raises rates. The consumer may oppose the increase but the ordinary citizen rarely is heard and seldom is mentioned in highly technical proceedings on the merits of proposed utility-rate requests.

But in Indiana, the consumer has a voice. The state pays a full-time attorney and two assistants to speak up for people in all utility proceedings. Known as the public counselor, this Hoosier official is an *ombudsman* whose advocacy focuses on utility rates and the quality of service.

The Indiana counselor is independent of the government body whose decisions he often appeals. However, the counselor is entitled to examine the records and utilize the staff of that agency, the Public Service Commission, which regulates utilities, including commuter-train service.

Carl Van Dorn, 40, who moved from the counselor's office in Indianapolis to a judge's appointment in Kokomo in 1974, concedes his job often was frustrating. "We didn't have the funding to match any single major utility, with its whole staff of experts, much less all the utilities in the state," he says. "But were there watching, making them prove their case, making them know at least the commission's minimum requirements were going to be maintained."

Though the state-supported opposition may be rudimental, its existence makes Indiana a leader in utility consumerism. Only one other state, Maryland, has a similar office. Several other states, including Massachusetts and Hawaii, have consumer councils or ombudsmen who handle utility problems along with many other duties. Legislators in Ohio and Montana are considering establishing an office similar to Indiana's.

The concept of a people's advocate in utility proceedings has gained support as the emerging energy crisis and new environmental priorities heighten the public's stake in how a utility runs its business. Furthermore, the unprecedented frequency of requested rate hikes has overburdened the state commissions; their abilities to fully investigate complex claims of many utilities diminishes as the volume of rate-increase requests increases.

In Indiana, for example, the Indiana Bell Telephone Co. had filed for substantial rate increases in each of the years 1969 through 1972. Counselor Van Dorn during 1973 presented arguments against a $35 million boost that would include the first 20-cent pay phone charges in the country. Indiana Bell obtained a $13,215,002 increase in 1972, $23,950,000 in 1971, and $10,880,000 in 1970.

When Indiana Bell filed the last request in December 1972, the company asked the Indiana Public Service Commission to grant $1.7 million in higher connection fees in a separate, emergency action to become effective in 30 days with no hearing. Van Dorn adamantly and successfully opposed the special treatment. So at least for a few months, Indiana consumers were spared an increase in installation charges to $20 from $15. And Indiana Bell's proposal to raise the fee to $25 was subject to hearings it sought to avoid by the special filing. In the end Indiana Bell received about three-fourths of its $35 million request.

Fighting Increases in Utility Bills

Van Dorn believes his participation led to a $1.6 million reduction in a general rate increase requested in 1972 by Indiana Bell.

Van Dorn and his assistant John Metts concede that most of their victories have involved smaller utilities. Metts recalls an Ohio Valley Gas Co. case he fought in 1970: The commission awarded only $375,000 of a requested $872,000 increase. In 1972 the commission rejected the entire $700,000 request of Public Telephone Co. of Southwest Indiana after Van Dorn emphasized it had based its case on the value of buildings not yet constructed.

In opposing the larger utilities with their large staffs of experts, Van Dorn and Metts say they could do little beyond picking at the weak points in each case. Van Dorn believes the office would be much more effective with a rate analyst, accountant, and engineer in order to challenge business practices and the way utilities plan to allocate charges. For example, many industrial users pay much less per unit of power than residential customers in Indiana and throughout the country. Before leaving the post, Van Dorn was successful in obtaining new state funds to bring more expertise to the office, boosting the annual budget to approximately $140,000.

He feels this is indicative of increased support of the governor and in the state. Van Dorn notes that during rate proceedings he tried to refine company regulations on deposits, discounting service, and other matters that affect consumers. "I took more time than a lot of people like if these rules seem improper or vague," says the soft-spoken Van Dorn. "I wanted to get into the record exactly how they are going to be interpreted."

As public counselor, Van Dorn also acted as a mediator in legal disputes. For example, he objected several times when a utility disconnected a customer's service because a relative failed to pay his bill. However, most complaints on billing and service are handled by a department of the Public Service Commission.

Easy-going Van Dorn seems to view his representation of Indiana consumers as a quiet matter of principle. Across the country in Bethesda, Md., People's Counsel Martin Freeman shows greater relish for battling the utilities.

Freeman, 32, tells of hiring a private-detective agency last year to observe 30 crews employed by Potomac Electric Power Co. in the Maryland suburbs of Washington, D.C. Freeman says the detective filmed workers standing idle or sleeping on the job. "A time study showed 47 per cent of their time was nonproductive, not counting the lunch hour and a couple of breaks," he says. "Crews were assigned to a major thoroughfare at 8:30 [a.m.] when ordinances prohibit work before 10:30, and three of four crews were assigned to the same job."

As a result of the investigation, Freeman says the Public Service Commission ordered the six large utilities in the state to first hire an outside consultant to conduct an efficiency study before applying for rate increases. If the consultant recommends measures a company declines to take, the commission indicates it may reduce its award by the amount it believes could have been saved.

Although Freeman spends only half of his work week as Maryland's people's counsel, he believes his efforts have brought substantial results. For the first time in the history of the Maryland commission, a rate case filed by a major utitlity was immediately dismissed. In 1972 the commission granted Freeman's motion to throw out a $40 million rate-increase request by the Chesapeake & Potomac Telephone Co. because too little time had elapsed since the last increase. "Nobody had ever thrown a major

21

utility out like that," Freeman says. "You could have cut the air in the hearing room with a knife."

In 1972 Baltimore Gas and Electric Co. asked for a $52 million increase. "The average homeowner would have had to pay a 16 per cent increase on his electric bill and a 5½ per cent increase on gas," Freeman recalls. Freeman argued that the company failed to achieve obtainable gains in productivity, and the commission granted only $15 million of the request.

Nationally, Sen. Lee Metcalf of Montana continues his battle of several years to set up a Federal agency of utility lawyers. Metcalf has introduced a bill to create an Office of Consumer's Counsel for Regulated Services that could intervene in all transportation and utility cases before Federal bodies. The agency could step into state hearings at the request of state officials and commissions or if petitioned by utility customers. Utilities would be required to furnish the agency with details on all facets of management and operations.

ACCIDENTAL LOSS of property may now qualify as a casualty loss for Federal income-tax purposes. The loss must result from an event that is: identifiable; damaging to property; and sudden, unexpected, and unusual. Simple accidental loss, such as dropping a wristwatch somewhere, still does not qualify. But following a U.S. Tax Court ruling, the Internal Revenue Service has allowed a deduction for the loss of a diamond, which occurred when a car door was slammed on a woman's hand, breaking the setting flanges on her ring. When the woman shook her hand in pain, the diamond dropped out and was never found. Only the part of an allowable loss in excess of $100 may be claimed for tax purposes.

HEALTH INSURANCE and roof coating are discussed in two new pamphlets published by the Council of Better Business Bureaus, Inc. "Facts about Health Insurance" explains the five types of health coverage, defines some confusing insurance terms in easily understood language, and provides guidelines to help evaluate individual health-insurance needs. "Tips on Roof Coatings" discusses advantages and disadvantages of materials used to patch or coat flat or low-pitch roof and includes a check list on roof maintenance. Single copies of both booklets are available free. Send a self-addressed, stamped envelope to the Council of Better Business Bureaus, Publications Department, 1150 17th St. N.W., Washington, D.C. 20036. The health-insurance booklet requires 20 cents in postage.

Escaping a Home Fire

FIRE woke a father of six at 4 a.m. in Willoughby, Ohio, not long ago. Finding smoke on the first floor, he immediately ran to the basement for a garden hose. Returning up the basement stairs, he found the first floor engulfed in flames and the passage upstairs blocked. From a neighbor's house he called the nearby fire department, which arrived quickly and extinguished the flames before they reached the bedrooms. The firemen found the man's wife and four of his children dead, killed by heat and toxic gases.

If people knew how to react to a fire in the home, this sort of thing wouldn't happen so often. There are about 700,000 fires in residences annually, causing about 6,600 deaths and more than $800 million in property damage. The suffering by those who are burned and survive—and by the uninjured kin of the dead—is not reducible to dollars or numbers.

Ignorance and panic most often kill occupants of a burning house. For example, the natural reaction is to sit or jump out of bed when aroused by the smell of smoke. That could be a mistake. Heat generated by the fire might be an endurable 125 degrees at bed level; the temperature a few feet above the bed could be 250 degrees, hot enough under some circumstances to knock you out immediately. Fire fighters suggest rolling from bed onto the floor, where temperatures are lowest.

Those who fight or prevent fires know a lot about surviving a fire. Knowing what they know can increase greatly the chances that you and your family will be able to get out of a burning house.

Some basic facts about home fires:

Most of them occur at night, between midnight and 6 a.m. When you're asleep, so are your senses, which may not detect a fire until it is raging.

A fire can spread killing heat and toxic gases through a house in an incredibly short time. About a minute after a fire starts, parts of a room under some circumstances may become as hot as 1,000 degrees. A few minutes more and the entire room's temperature will reach 700 degrees, causing all combustible material to burst spontaneously into flames. Almost all materials found in the home give off toxic gases—mostly carbon monoxide—when they are burning. The heat and gases, which will reach the home's upper floors far ahead of the flames, are responsible for most deaths.

How much time do you have to get out? The National Fire Protection Association gives the following estimates of escape time available from the time a fire is burning well in the living room until intolerable conditions reach the bedrooms:

If the home's interior finish is combustible and if the bedroom doors are open, you have 1.8 minutes; with closed bedroom doors, 5.6 minutes (closed doors slow down the spread of a fire's smoke and gases). With non-combustible interior finish and open doors, 2.5 minutes; with closed doors, 11.7 minutes.

If you and your family do not know exactly what to do once an established fire is discovered, the chances are someone will not get out. Forget those movies in which a brave parent fights flames and smoke to save the family:

Escaping a Home Fire

There are too many real-life stories of parents who ran into hot, smoke-filled hallways to save their children and were found dead on the floor, felled by heat and poisonous gas.

To survive a home fire, a family should have an escape plan that is understood by all members and has been practiced in drills.

Here's how to devise an escape plan:

First, draw a floor plan of sleeping quarters, indicating stairways, all windows, and ledges or garage roofs onto which occupants can escape.

The occupants of each room should have two escape routes.

The first route is through the door if that's possible. To determine in a fire whether the hallway is passable, fire fighters suggest feeling the inside of your closed bedroom door, preferably near the top where the heat gathers; or feel a metal doorknob, which is a good heat conductor. If the door feels hot, forget the hallway; you probably won't survive the intense heat and gas on the other side. If the door is cool, check the hall by bracing yourself against the door, turning your head to the side, and opening slowly.

One must have an alternative way out of the bedroom if the hallway is impassable. Climbing out a first-floor window is easy. On higher floors, if possible select an escape window over a ledge or roof, where a person could stay until help arrives. When no ledge is nearby, you might equip the room with a collapsible ladder or a heavy rope tied to a strong hook that fits over the window ledge.

An escape plan should also include:

● A common fire warning: Yelling "fire" is one way; another is to put a shrill policeman's or sports official's whistle in each room.

● An outside meeting place: Everyone should meet in one spot. People have been killed going back into a burning building to rescue someone already out of it.

● Assigned jobs: Once outside, someone should have the job of calling the fire department. Someone else should circle the house to check for the missing. If there are infants or elderly persons in the home, someone should be responsible for getting a ladder up to their room, if they are missing. (Remember: You have a better chance of saving a person by entering a room from the outside than you have of making it through a superheated hallway.)

● If anyone is missing when the fire department arrives, each family member should be able to tell the firemen exactly where in the house the missing person should be.

One reason a good escape plan is so necessary is that a person close to or in the midst of a large fire tends to become irrational, and a parent's panic may cause needless deaths. The cause of the panic and irrationality is as much physical as psychological. Carbon monoxide, present in almost any home fire, will weaken muscles and slow down nervous reactions when inhaled. Knowing what to do ahead of time will make instinctive reactions easier. Here are some more fire-survival tips:

✔ Sleep with bedroom doors closed; they'll hold out heat and gas longer.

✔ Keep low when escaping through the house or moving about your room, and cover your face with a cloth, wetted if possible.

✔ If you lose your sight and orientation in a smoke-filled room, go to the wall and move around it, feeling for a window.

✔ Don't be panicked into jumping from a window; a

long jump can kill you as surely as the fire, and fire departments generally respond quickly. If trapped, stuff up the crack between the door and floor with clothing or towels. Open a top window slightly to let bad air escape. Then open the bottom window and straddle the sill with your head leaning out; if you fall, you'll fall out, not in. Don't jump until the heat becomes unbearable, and when you do jump, aim for bushes or shrubbery to break the fall.

What about home fire-alarm systems? Some fire fighters feel a good detection system is the best possible protection one can have. Unfortunately, telling a good alarm from a bad one isn't easy.

The National Bureau of Standards is studying various detection devices, hoping to establish standards for Federally constructed buildings. "The range of quality in detectors is extreme," says George Sinnott of the bureau. "Some are quite good, others are essentially worthless." Sinnott, however, says he is not free to identify by brand the good and bad systems he has examined.

There are two popular types of detection systems: One detects heat, the other detects smoke. Sinnott advised against buying a heat detector because gases and smoke generally precede a fire's high temperatures. A sophisticated smoke detector may cost between $50 and $100. Before buying one, be sure it has the Underwriters Laboratories "UL" seal of approval. A good system will detect very slight changes in hallway atmosphere caused by fire smoke. When it detects smoke, the device will set off either a loud horn or ringing bell.

Richard Bland, head of the National Commission on Fire Prevention and Control, says, "We feel that if you put a smoke detector in the hall, you'll increase your survival chance by about 95 per cent." Bland says a detector "won't stop your house from burning down, but it'll alert you your home is on fire."

None of these escape and protection procedures will do much good unless everyone in the family is familiar and comfortable with them. Schools, hospitals, and offices stage periodic fire drills. Do the same in your home. The fire experts suggest, though, that you don't make them too scary, or young children might freeze up during a real fire.

Dangers in Mobile Homes

ONE of every 27 Americans lives in a mobile home. Or to put it another way, mobile homes house a population nearly equal to New York City's.

In hard figures, this is 7,750,000 persons. They live in 3,400,000 dwellings that have rolled out of factories in Indiana, Michigan, California, and Virginia, then along highways, finally coming to rest (minus wheels, but with skirts) in thousands of trailer parks, usually tucked away out of sight in woods and fields on the far fringes of metropolitan areas.

Of all single-family homes built in 1973, 40 per cent were mobile homes. Of all new homes that cost $20,000 or under, more than three-fourths were mobile homes.

These homes are compact, cheap, furnished, relatively maintenance free, and yard free. They're good beginnings for the newly married; good endings for the retired.

These homes also are the deadliest homes built in America. The reason is fire. For years, the mobile-home industry has been jousting with safety critics, only slowly changing materials to make these lightweight, plywood-based homes safer. Now, the industry is under its severest assault ever. Again, the reason is a fire, one that took eight lives on Christmas Eve in 1973 near Flint, Michigan.

The dead were Paul Hartman, 32; his wife, Phyllis, 29; Mrs. Hartman's four children by a previous marriage; a live-in baby sitter; and the baby sitter's infant daughter.

Investigators suspect a gas furnace overheated and melted.

Three days after the fire, Genesee County Prosecutor Robert F. Leonard gave the case to a grand jury. Said Leonard: "The investigation will be concerned with the possible gross negligence of the mobile-home industry, who knowingly placed in the stream of commerce of this state dangerous instrumentalities which they know or should know will unnecessarily expose mobile-home residents to serious bodily harm or death if fire occurs."

The consumer-conscious Michigan prosecutor called mobile homes "tinder boxes." He said the 800,000 Michigan residents who live in such homes "are flirting with imminent disaster by residing in totally unsafe and highly combustible mobile homes.

Subpoenas have been issued to more than a dozen persons, nationwide, in the mobile-home industry. Under pressure from Leonard's office, Michigan has announced emergency safety measures governing construction of all new mobile homes sold in the state.

Though Michigan is one of only seven states that has failed to adopt all or part of an industry safety code, Leonard has chosen to tackle the entire multibillion-dollar industry.

"We recognize it's going to cost [consumers] more money," said Leonard. "But money has to be an insignificant factor in this when lives are at stake. I think mobile homes can be built more safely, and at a profit. This is one of the fastest growing industries in the country, and it has one of the highest profits because of the very cheap building materials."

In 1973 the nation's 350 mobile-home makers shipped 575,000 units, worth $4 billion, according to the

Mobile Home Manufacturer's Association, Chantilly, Va.

This group, of course, disputes Leonard's view on the mobile home as a fire hazard. Says John Martin, president of the industry association: "We're trying to bring out that our fire record nationwide is better than other residential units. Leonard cannot prove that 9 out of 10 mobile homes in Michigan are firetraps. He has no supporting evidence for making such a judgment on fire safety."

Indeed, statistics on mobile-home fires are scanty. Only 11 states bother to compile them. In a book to be published later this year by the Center for Auto Safety, a Nader group in Washington, D.C., author Lynda McDonnell reports that "the incidence of fire in one- and two-family conventional homes was about the same as in mobile homes," according to one study. But she also quotes an Oregon study that shows that "the fatality rate for mobile home fires was 2.3 times greater than that for conventional homes.

The nub of the argument by critics such as McDonnell and Leonard is that, unlike conventional homes, when a fire breaks out in a mobile home, the loss usually is total. Because of its compactness, the materials used, and the way it's built, a mobile home usually burns up in minutes.

The mobile-home makers are paying for a study by the National Bureau of Standards to find out what does happen when fire breaks out in mobile homes.

At issue is whether the standards of the code developed by the American National Standards Institute and the National Fire Protection Association used by the industry are adequate. Martin, the chief of the mobile-home makers' group, acknowledges they are minimum standards. Leonard and McDonnell say they are inadequate.

The Hartman trailer, for example, was only six months old and met the institute standards.

Critics contend the institute standards aren't strict enough on wiring and installation of furnaces and make no mention of the use of heat tapes. The tapes are insulation used to protect pipes attached under trailers and exposed to winter weather. The industry says heat tapes are mobile homeowners' responsibility, not the builders.

McDonnell says furnaces in mobile homes are installed in hallway closets, with little or no clearance between the heating units and wooden walls. She also feels that the institute code on the speed with which flames can spread on test pieces of wood is inadequate. "Mobile-home floors . . . are generally made of chipboard or particle board, inexpensive sheets composed of compressed wood chips, sawdust, and glue," she says in her forthcoming book. "Mobile-home ceilings, although sometimes made of gypsum, are more often . . . a fiberboard made of wood pulp and plant fibers. Both fiberboard ceilings and chipboard floors contribute to rapid flame spread."

McDonnell also says that more than 250 pounds of plastic is used in each mobile home for pipes, cabinets, furniture, cushioning, rugs, drapes, and bed spreads. Many items, she says, are "not treated with fire retardants." She warns: "Exactly how severe the fire hazard of plastic building materials and furniture is has not yet been answered."

"Most of these things to improve safety can be done overnight at the factory," says Leonard. Addition of smoke detectors, under 1973 revised institute standards, was easy, he said. He acknowledges that mobile homes do offer low-cost housing to persons otherwise unable to afford it, but adds, "Sometimes we have to protect people against themselves. Maybe we ought to have a moratorium on the sale of mobile homes."

McDonnell, the Nader investigator, says, "A lot of states are waiting for some sort of Federal legislation because they feel incapable themselves of solving the problems" of tougher mobile-home standards.

Robert Myers is president of the Michigan Mobile Homeowners Association in Ypsilanti. At a meeting here called by the mobile-home makers, Myers listened to the industry defend its safety record, and believed very little of what he heard.

"Our constitution requires me to live in a mobile home," he said "They're not safe. I'm a gambler. I'm gambling I won't die."

Because of mobile homes' vulnerability to fire, says Paul Miller, chief of the consumer-protection division of the prosecuting attorney's office of Genesee County, Michigan, these safety precautions should be observed by mobile-home residents:

(1) Install a smoke detector.

(2) If wall electric outlets are warm to the touch, call an electrician immediately.

3) Never use a fuse rated higher than the one called for in the electrical system.

(4) Use extension cords sparingly to avoid overloading the electrical system.

(5) Check furnace filter often; clean when dirty to avoid overheating furnace motor.

(6) Do not install bypasses on "limit switches" on furnaces to provide increased heat.

(7) High thermostat settings (80 to 85 degrees) to keep drafty mobile homes warm force a furnace to run continuously and may cause the blower to overheat and fail.

(8) Do not add rooms to a mobile home without making sure the furnace can provide the additional heat needed.

(9) Do not store flammable objects in furnace or water-heater areas or under the trailer.

(10) Keep fire extinguisher handy.

(11) Keep a hatchet handy in homes without "kick-out" windows.

(12) Do not seal doors to keep out the cold.

(13) Make sure children know emergency escape routes.

Are Aerosols Safe Enough?

WHEN archeologists in some distant age excavate the remains of current civilization, chances are they'll quickly uncover one of its hallmarks: the aerosol can. From deodorants and cheese spreads to oven cleaners and spray paint, hundreds of products now are available in aerosol sprays. Consumers snap up about three billion of these neat, convenient, supposedly safe cans yearly.

But, scientists, public-interest groups, and Government agencies have been taking a new look at aerosols and asking whether they are as safe as is commonly believed. Some consumers, they suggest, may be getting more than they bargain for in the form of harmful immediate and long-term side effects. While the allegations have drawn a sharp rebuttal from the industry, many of the critics' questions remain unanswered.

The basic question being raised about aerosols is whether their extra convenience is worth extra risks and extra costs. In a strictly economic sense, consumers usually fare less well with aerosols than with other types of dispensers. As a 1969 report on packaging by the Environmental Protection Agency states, "The price of any product in an aerosol container is considerably higher than that of the same product in any other container." This is so because of the extra costs of aerosol packaging: strong-walled containers, valves, solvents to dissolve the product, and propellants to spray it.

Only in the past few years, however, has the safety of aerosols been questioned. Teen-agers trying to get "high" by inhaling large amounts of aerosol sprays set off an inquiry in the late 1960s. Many of the young people died, the victims of sudden heart failure, and investigations into their deaths revealed the the ingredients giving them their "highs"—primarily the propellants used to produce aerosol sprays—were also causing their hearts to stop beating. While recognizing that their deaths were caused by aerosol misuse, researchers began asking whether normal aerosol use might pose dangers, particularly to persons with heart problems.

Privately financed public-interest groups began to follow the lead of such researchers. Since 1973, three groups—the Center for Science in the Public Interest, Center for Concerned Engineering, and Health Research Group—have issued reports alleging dangers of aerosols and calling for stricter regulation by the Federal Government.

The Government appears to be listening. One of the first acts of the Consumer Product Safety Commission, created in 1973, was to ban the sale of adhesive sprays on the suspicion that they caused birth defects. The commission rescinded the ban after further investigation failed to show a cause-effect relationship. But shortly thereafter, in response to a petition from the Center for Science in the Public Interest, the commission held two days of hearings on aerosol products as a class. The commission is now analyzing the results of those hearings.

The Food and Drug Administration (FDA), meanwhile, is preparing new requirements for cautionary labeling on several types of aerosol drugs and cosmetics and has recalled two brands of asthma sprays and six brands of cough sprays (the cough-spray recall followed 21 deaths attributed to a solvent in the spray Pertussin).

Critics allege three major risks associated with the use of aerosols:

● Their pressurized containers may explode when exposed to heat, spewing shrapnel and chemicals onto nearby persons. Children and adults have been seriously injured and even killed by cans accidentally thrown in burning trash. Cans have occasionally exploded when left inside cars parked in hot sunlight.

● The inhaled propellant, usually freon gas, may be toxic not only to "sniffers" seeking a "high" but, under some circumstances, to persons using aerosols slightly higher than normal concentrations. Some data indicate that heart patients and asthmatics may be particularly vulnerable. In addition, not enough is known about long-term effects; some studies indicate damage to the lungs, liver, and other organs.

● A product's active ingredients, which may be reasonably safe in other forms, may be dangerous when inhaled as an aerosol mist. For example, the lye in some oven cleaners, when sprayed as a mist, may settle as minute particles on eyes, enter the lungs and bloodstream, and reach all organs of the body. The effects of such body penetration are not known.

The aerosol industry flatly rejects such accusations. Its Aerosol Education Bureau, based in New York City, acknowledges that deliberate misuse of aerosol products "as in sniffing concentrated vapors to get high" can be fatal, but emphasizes that all available evidence indicates aerosols are safe in normal use, including closed quarters such as bathrooms. The industry is continuing to conduct research on the potential toxicity of aerosols, a spokesman says. But he notes, "We've all been using aerosols for over 20 years, and that is some indication of their safety." Dr. Robert Giovacchini, chairman of the industry's aerosol safety committee, testified in Consumer Product Safety Commission's hearings that the few studies indicating aerosols are unsafe do not hold up to scientific scrutiny. Deaths associated with the Pertussin, he said, were due to "gross misuse of the vaporizer."

Industry spokesmen also attribute aerosol injuries to carelessness and "product abuse," and note that all aerosol products contain warnings against exposure to high temperatures, puncturing, excessive inhalation, and other misuse. Very few injuries have occurred, considering the large number of aerosols in use, they contend.

Members of the public-interest groups challenging aerosols reply that warning labels are not enough. "How many people really pay attention to these warnings?" asks Albert Fritsch, a chemist and codirector of the Center for Science in the Public Interest. "How many small children read them?"

Fritsch's group has asked the Commission on Product Safety, a Federal Agency, to conduct a public-education program on the dangers of aerosol sprays used in the home, to ban toxic and unsafe aerosol products, and to test aerosols for long-term side effects. Until such tests are complete, the group has asked the commission to require manufacturers to adopt child-proof caps and explosion proof containers.

The public-interest critics may get some of what they ask. At hearings, the commissioners seemed sympathetic to their concerns and perplexed by some of the industry's explanations. Chairman Richard Simpson disputed the industry's figures showing few aerosol injuries, saying that reports from the commission's National Electronic Injury Surveillance System indicate there were about

12,000 aerosol-related injuries in the United States in 1973.

Before it makes its decision, however, the commission will have to answer a question posed repeatedly by Simpson: "Is the extra convenience of aerosols worth even a few injuries or deaths, considering the products are available in other forms?"

Relax and Live Longer

YOU'VE kicked your pack-a-day cigaret habit. You've changed your diet, and now your weight is normal and your cholesterol count is below 200. You've even gotten the happy word from your doctor that your blood pressure is a healthy 120 over 80.

So is there anything else you can do to reduce the risk that you'll die of an early heart attack? Well, try asessing your personality:

● Do you fret that you are always falling behind in the things you should or could do, and do you try to do more and more things in less and less time?

● Do you become highly irritated when you aren't seated in a restaurant immediately, or when your plane is delayed, or when traffic holds you up?

● Are you so competitive that you get angry when a child beats you at a game?

● Do you clench your jaws tightly when thinking and your fists during ordinary conversations?

● Are even your most relaxed discussions studded with curse words?

If that sounds like the real you, research at Mount Zion Hospital and Medical Center in San Francisco suggests you are a heart attack waiting to happen.

Since 1959 Dr. Meyer Friedman and Dr. Ray Rosenman—director and associate director, respectively, of Mount Zion's Harold Brunn Institute—have studied the relationship between personality and heart disease.

41

They've concluded it is a major factor in heart attacks—indeed, *the* major factor for people under 60—more important than obesity, high blood pressure, elevated cholesterol, and even cigaret smoking.

The two cardiologists have dubbed people whose personality traits put them at highest risk "Type A," and those at lowest risk "Type B." "We believe the evidence we have and are obtaining points more and more closely to a direct causal relationship between Type A behavior pattern and coronary heart disease," says Friedman. "At least 90 per cent of all patients having heart attacks under age 60, we've found, exhibit Type A behavior pattern."

The two doctors see America's life-styles as the key to its soaring rate of heart disease. They say it is the pace and demands of modern living, and the way people respond to them, that account for so many heart attacks among the young and middle-aged, particularly men.

Too often, they argue, the most likely candidate for a coronary is the doer-shaker-mover-achiever who relentlessly pursues the "American Dream" of success, status, and material well-being. And this means that heart disease involves psychological, social, and environmental factors previously unexplored. "The physician must look at the patient as well as his cholesterol," says Friedman.

The Friedman-Rosenman concept is far from universally accepted; many doctors regard their findings as interesting, but not conclusive. "Although now there's much cocktail conversation about Type As and Type Bs at medical meetings, it is not without a humorous, 'Do you believe it or not?' tone," says Dr. Samuel Fox III, former president of the American College of Cardiology.

Nonetheless, the idea that a life-style and its stresses can be a factor in heart disease is winning converts as other researchers confirm the Mount Zion statistical and biochemical findings.

Fox personally finds the evidence persuasive. "The setting of a person's sights on his life-style may prove to be as important [for heart patients] as some of our surgical techniques," he says.

Most Americans are a combination of Type A and Type B behavior patterns; the greater the Type A behavior, the greater the risk. Friedman and Rosenman estimate that 10 per cent of urban males are pure Type A and 10 per cent pure Type B. Women, says Friedman, are more often Type Bs. "By custom they are not put in a socioeconomic milieu that encourages speed and aggression," he explains.

But as times change, so does the role of women in society, and women's lib may produce a corresponding jump in heart attacks among women. "Ever since Mac-Arthur liberated the Japanese woman, her coronary-artery disease has increased fourfold," says Friedman.

The two researchers began examining the role of personality in heart disease in the late 1950s, because of the chiding of a woman helping them in another study. At that time they were interested in cholesterol as a factor in heart attacks.

With the co-operation of a women's club, they tried to determine if the higher cholesterol levels in men resulted because they ate different foods than their wives. The study showed the diets were basically the same. The club president then suggested the two doctors look at what was really killing off males—the way they drove themselves.

In 1960 and 1960 the Mount Zion team screened 3,524 male volunteers aged 39 to 59 and classified them by personality types. Some 3,000 of them were kept track of for up to 8½ years.

It was in this study that Type A personalities accounted for 90 per cent of the heart attacks among men under 60. Moreover, the researchers found that among males of all ages, Type As have 2½ times as many heart attacks as Type Bs; an A's coronary is twice as likely to be fatal; and As who survive their first heart attack have five times the risk of suffering a second. Even more surprising, Type As who never smoked cigarets had nearly twice the heart-attack rate of Type Bs who smoked about a pack a day.

The researchers use a series of questions to aid them in classifying personality types. But they find that how questions are answered—the tone of voice, volume, physical movements, and expressions—is a better indicator than the answers themselves. For this reason, classifications are made only after interviews by trained personnel.

The classic Type A personality—the really high-risk individual—is hurried, impatient, constantly under stress from an urgent, pressing feeling that he hasn't enough time. His body movements are brisk. His fists are frequently clenched. He speaks in explosive, hurried speech, and his body seems always tense, never relaxed.

Friedman describes a Type A individual as obsessed with numbers—of sales made, of articles written, of forms completed, of letters filed. They are often snappish, angry, irritated, and prone to vent their hostility in verbal abuse on family, friends, associates, and even strangers.

"They are always overdriving," says Friedman. "The two characteristics of Type A behavior are 'hurry sickness' and 'free-floating hostility.'" Such individuals are in what he calls "a chronic, continuous struggle."

"Whenever a man struggles too incessantly to accomplish too many things in too little a space of time, thus engendering in himself a sense of time urgency, or whenever a man struggles too competitively with other individuals, this struggle markedly accentuates the course of coronary-heart disease," Friedman wrote in the Yale Alumni Journal. "If this struggle is not abated, I suspect that it does little good to alter one's diet, smoking, or exercise habits, because the biochemical forces generated by this internal unrest are quite capable in themselves of bringing on the *denouement* of cardiac arrest."

Neither researcher argues that exercising moderately and controlling weight, high blood pressure, and high cholesterol aren't important. But they do say that these efforts are not enough.

Type A personalities are not restricted to hard-driving, success-oriented executives. The behavior pattern is more a state of mind than station in life. "There are plenty of As among truck drivers," says Friedman.

Type B people, by definition, have personalities that are opposite of Type As. This doesn't mean they are incapable of hard work, achievement, and advancing to lofty positions. In Friedman's view, they generally make better executives because they don't rush decisions, make snap judgments, or antagonize their subordinates.

"The fundamental difference between the A and B types is that the B knows precisely how good he is," says Friedman. "He knows his capabilities and he knows his limitations. The A doesn't, and doesn't wish to.

Type As abound, says Friedman, among trial lawyers, TV performers, salesmen, auto racers, and newspaper reporters. There seem to be more Type Bs among patent attorneys, government clerks, accountants, and embalmers.

The Mount Zion researchers can't say precisely what

produces a Type A personality. But they suspect that parental and social expectations play a large role, producing the psychological pressures that result in hurry sickness and free-floating hostility.

Western society encourages Type A behavior by offering special rewards to those who can think, perform, communicate, and conduct their affairs more quickly and more aggressively than others. Most parents want their children to succeed, so they encourage, even force them to compete in school and outside. Psychiatrists say some people spend their lifetimes trying to live up to impossible expectations instilled in them by their parents.

And the quest for material possessions, fostered so forcefully by advertising campaigns, often leads men to work exhausting hours as they strive for "the good things in life"—a vacation home, a recreational vehicle, a larger boat and motor.

"The stress has become almost unbearable," says Friedman. "Everybody is selling his time for money. Many parole officers tell me that one thing they have to do is acclimate long-term prisoners to this increased pace of society when they are released."

Type A behavior, then, is an outward expression of inner turmoil and desires. But Friedman, Rosenman, and their Mount Zion colleagues have found that stresses afflicting Type As apparently produce major and important physical changes as well—changes that may explain why they are far more susceptible to heart attacks.

Early in their work Friedman and Rosenman showed that the stress and tension engendered by deadline pressures can send cholesterol levels soaring. They took two groups of tax accountants—most of whom fell midway in the A-B spectrum—and measured their blood cholesterol levels over six months, beginning in January. The first group had two tax deadlines, one in January and the other on April 15. The second group had only the April deadline. Cholesterol counts in both groups shot up shortly before the April deadline; but in January only the group with a tax deadline showed cholesterol increases.

That was the beginning. Now, Friedman reports, the group has found that Type As have high cholesterol; increased norepinephrine, a vital chemical of the nervous system; an overabundance of insulin; increased ACTH, a hormone that stimulates the adrenal glands; and low levels of growth hormone. Also, their blood clots faster than normal, and autopsy studies show Type As average twice as much hardening of the arteries as Type Bs.

"We think high cholesterol is an indicator of Type A behavior," says Friedman. "It's very rare to have a Type B have a high cholesterol rate."

Friedman acknowledges there is no scientific evidence as yet that changing a person's behavior will prolong his life, although the Mount Zion team is now organizing a study attempt to find out. All that exists is clinical impressions, the personal observations of Mount Zion (and other) doctors that people who do change lengthen and improve the quality of their lives.

Friedman himself suffered a mild heart attack in 1966. The attack left him pondering his future. With some effort, he says, he managed to change his Type A behavior through what he calls "re-engineering" and others call behavior modification.

He and Rosenman have written a book for laymen titled *Type A Behavior and Your Heart*. In it they outline some steps to help those who want to change.

Curing hurry sickness is important, and part of this is realizing that relaxation is not a luxury but a necessity. They urge eliminating unnecessary events and activities;

getting up 15 minutes early to give more time to dress and talk with the family; slowing down your pace of eating and drinking; and taking time alone to read, dream, and analyze your life.

They also suggest reminding yourself that life remains unfinished. Only death finishes things up, and even then, if you lived an extra day, there would still be things you would do. As you sweat over something, says Friedman, ask yourself if it's really going to make a difference in your life five years from now.

A major characteristic of Type As, says Friedman, is "polyphasic thinking," trying to do more than one thing at a time. He tells of a chemist, "a real Type A," who would shave, read, and eat all at once. The man died of a heart attack in his early 50s.

So the two researchers urge doing one thing at a time. "Remember," they write, "that even Einstein, when tying his shoelaces, thought chiefly about the bow." Make an effort to pay atention to people—particularly your family. Focus on what they are saying; don't let your mind wander.

If you find something you are doing tends to induce tension—writing reports, balancing your checkbook, ironing—take short breaks. And if a particular individual constantly angers you, find ways to avoid him or her.

Perhaps the best thing to do about hostility is to keep reminding yourself you're hostile, Friedman says. This is a forewarned-is-forearmed approach. The thought will surface in your mind as your temper rises, and help you realize what's happening. Then you can check your outburst.

If all this sounds a bit like pop psychology, well, in a way it is. And if it seems rather hard to apply in real life, it is that too. Friedman acknowledges changing behavior patterns takes effort and more effort—"drill," he calls it.

But the alternative, Friedman suggests, is even more unpleasant. "If you don't change your Type A behavior pattern, you have absolutely no protection against coronary heart disease," he says.

Sometimes it's hard to tell whether a patient has in fact had a heart attack. The attack may be mild, and evidence confirming the attack doesn't show up in the blood for at least 12 hours.

But a new test that can detect evidence of a heart attack within a few hours has been developed by Doctors Stanley H. Bernstein and Harry Saranchak of Mt. Sinai Hospital in Hartford, Conn. They test the patient's urine to see if it contains myoglobin, an oxygen-carrying protein that's usually found in heart-muscle cells. This protein leaks into the bloodstream and quickly into the urine after the heart muscle is damaged, as it is in a heart attack. Myoglobin isn't found in healthy persons' urine.

Myoglobin can be detected in urine as long as four days after a heart attack, a day or two longer than evidence of an attack can be found in the blood using present blood-enzyme tests. This can be significant for someone who suffers a mild attack but doesn't seek medical help for a few days.

The two physicians are simplifying their test so it can be done at bedside or in a doctor's office. Now it can be done easily only in a laboratory.

Spotting
Injury-Causing Hazards

A man and a woman knocked purposefully at the front door of a brick home in suburban northern Virginia, flashed identification to a woman who answered, and began an inquiry that soon would yield crucial evidence: a paint-thinner can, a scrap of burned cloth, and a singed shoelace.

The evidence will help solve another who-done-it or, more precisely, what-done-it. An accident rather than a crime prompted the visit. The two callers are employees of the Injury Data and Control Center, a division of the U.S. Consumer Product Safety Commission in Bethesda, Md. The Commission attempts to reduce frequency and severity of injuries involving consumer goods by collecting accident information and using it to develop new product tests and standards and consumer-education programs.

The investigators came to the home of Lt. Col. and Mrs. Kenneth Kellogg to determine how their son Randy, 12, had seriously burned his legs. The injury-data center learned of his accident through a teleprinter linking its computer with Fairfax Hospital, where Randy was treated.

Fairfax is one of 119 hospitals in the bureau's National Electronic Injury Surveillance System (NEISS), which has been operational since 1972. Each hospital transmits to the center data on all emergency-room patients who are killed or injured in accidents involving products.

50

Every year there are some 20 million such accidents, which kill 30,000 Americans, the commission estimates. Many of the survivors are disabled for the rest of their lives. Many are children who must undergo painful medical treatment and learn to live with scarred bodies.

Randy Kellogg, for example, needs extensive skin grafting that his mother says probably must be repeated as he grows. Investigators Jim Taylor and Cindy Bacon listened sympathetically, taking notes as Marjorie Kellogg told how her son and a friend has used paint thinner to light a fire in a lean-to "fort." Apparently vapors ignited and the can exploded in flames. Randy's inexpensive jeans quickly burned.

The investigators examined a pair of jeans that Mrs. Kellogg believes are identical to those that burned. They studied the high-topped boots that protected Randy's feet and extracted what remained of the partially burned shoelaces. Guided by Randy's older brother Curt, they tramped through the cold to the site of the fire and to a nearby dump, where they salvaged the paint-thinner can. They were jubilant when Curt found a scrap of Randy's burned jeans in the woods.

The cloth and the shoelace will be used in research on flammability of consumer products. Photographs of the can along with a lengthy report will be filed at the data center after Randy is released from the hospital. Eventually, information on his accident may contribute to new product standards to prevent similar injuries.

Such in-depth inquiries into accidents involving consumer products—from snowmobiles to fondue pots—are conducted throughout the country by 32 investigative units. Every day, at the direction of the injury-data center, teams follow up about 20 injuries treated in emergency rooms that are linked to the NEISS computer.

Initially, the center gets only a few essential facts on each injury. The consumer product that might be involved is the only item emergency rooms in the NEISS network add to routine admission queries. "We know people aren't there to participate in a Federal survey but to get treatment," says William V. White of the commission. He also emphasizes that no names or addresses are initially reported or kept in the center's files. To follow up an accident, the center must use a number to obtain the name from the hospital. Investigators destroy a form containing names and addresses when each case is closed. And the teams are sworn to maintain confidentiality, White says. (This writer was able to accompany the Taylor-Bacon team only after being identified as a journalist and receiving Mrs. Kellogg's permission to observe the investigation.)

The 119 NEISS hospitals treat about 38 per cent of all accident victims taken to hospitals and were chosen to provide a statistically representative sampling of all injuries handled in hospital emergency rooms. Thus, because 41 per cent of all NEISS-reported injuries involving glass containers are to the hand, the center assumes 41 per cent of all glass-container injuries are to the hand. The center says 8 per cent of all the injuries caused by gas furnaces are lacerations, rather than burns, so researchers look for sharp edges as well as heating problems in studying furnace design.

As a result of the center's research, the Consumer Product Safety Commission has achieved modification of several products that have caused injuries. For example, an investigative unit in Denver discovered that children were severely burned when they tipped over vaporizers containing scalding water. At the commission's suggestion, manufacturers in 1972 modified designs to reduce the temperature of all but a small amount of water in the vaporizer core, which a child can't reach.

The commission learned a child often suffers disfiguring electrical burns by putting an extension cord to his mouth. Beginning in 1973, Underwriters' Laboratories, Inc., a nonprofit, standard-setting corporation, required that a single extension cord contain no more than three outlets on its head and that two of those must bear an insulating insert that a child can't remove. By January 1975 all certified extension cords must be designed to join perfectly when plugged into other cords, thereby eliminating loose connections that cause burns.

Another modification, which took effect in 1973, will prevent containers used with certain types of food blenders from unlatching while in use. The commission learned that many consumers cut their fingers on the blades when they instinctively reach to steady the container.

Warning on Gasoline

IF you're tempted to start a gasoline siphon by sucking on it, don't. Medical experts warn that swallowing or inhaling gasoline has killed some persons and can cause pneumonia, heart problems, damage to internal organs, or depression of the central nervous system.

The greatest danger is the possibility of inhaling liquid gasoline into the lungs, says Dr. Sorell Schwartz, associate professor of pharmacology at Georgetown University in Washington, D.C. "This can cause rapid, severe, and fatal lung damage from very small amounts—even droplets—of gasoline," he says.

Schwartz believes it's most important to remember what *not* to do, instead of what to if a person ingests gasoline. He says a person tends to spit it out and then inhale deeply, a reaction that's likely to suck it into the lungs. Instead, a person should wash away the gasoline without taking any deep breaths.

If gasoline is swallowed, don't try to induce vomiting because of the risk of drawing the gasoline into the lungs, where it is much more toxic than in the stomach.

Above all, don't try to administer your own first aid, Schwartz warns. Seek medical help immediately.

Dr. Neil Solomon, Maryland secretary of health and mental hygiene, notes that a victim may neglect treatment because some siphoning accidents occur during gasoline theft. He says symptoms of untreated gasoline ingestion include headache, vomiting, nausea, vertigo, loss of co-ordination, mental confusion, convulsions, and distress in breathing.

If a small mechanical siphon is not available and you must siphon gasoline during an emergency, Solomon suggests using a clear plastic tube that at least allows a person to see the liquid so it does not enter the mouth.

Keep in mind that even gasoline vapors may have toxic effects. Schwartz, the Georgetown professor, says vapors can depress or slow down the central nervous system, sensitize the heart, causing irregular rhythms, and cause some lung damage.

The Mysteries of Allergies

AT first the ninth-grade girl resisted. But the gym instructor shouted, causing everyone to stare at her. So she started the physical-fitness exercises —and collapsed.

The 5-year-old began to balk at going to kindergarten. But the school psychologist talked to her, and her mother urged her. So the little girl went peaceably, only to return home sick each day.

Like Rick DeMont, the U.S. swimmer who was disqualified from the Munich Olympics as a consequence of taking asthma medicine that was mistakingly alleged to increase performance, the two girls have allergy-caused illnesses. Like Rick, they also fell victim to the ignorance and misunderstanding that routinely add hardship and misery to the discomfort or pain of numerous allergy-sick people.

Yet the allergy victim's lot may be improving, however slowly. The Government has expanded a major allergy-research program. Medical investigators have reported new findings and promised "exciting clinical [or treatment] gains" in two or three years. And volunteers, doctors, and school officials in Maryland's Montgomery County have undertaken a simple, novel, but potentially significant program that they hope could become a national model.

Such a program might have prevented the collapse of the asthmatic ninth-grader and saved from travail the preschooler, who is allergic to mold. For among other things, the plan suggests establishing alternate exercise programs for asthmatic youngsters. It calls for training maintenance supervisors to hunt for and eliminate allergens such as "the enormous growth of molds" the child's allergist found on and under the kindergarten carpeting.

If improvement for allergy sufferers hasn't come before, it hasn't been for lack of patients. More than 31 million people contend with allergy-created ailments. In fact, allergies cause the nation's most common chronic sicknesses.

Dr. Gilbert Barkin, a Silver Spring, Md., allergist and former regent of the American College of Allergists, says that allergy-caused conditions account for nearly a third of "all chronic conditions in children under 17 years of age" and force afflicted youngsters to miss a total of nine million "school days" annually. Allergy-affected adults annually lose a total of 9.5 million work days worth $250 million in salaries and wages, he adds.

Few realize it, but asthma, the most serious of the allergy-provoked diseases, kills roughly 5,000 persons yearly. According to Dr. Michael H. K. Irwin, a New York City allergist specializing in occupational medicine, asthma annually hospitalizes more than 134,000 people for average stays of nearly 10 days. Children make up a fourth of the hospitalized patients.

In general, asthma treatments consume as little as 2 per cent and as much as 30 per cent of victims' total incomes. The 13 million or more treated sufferers from hay fever pay more than $100 million a year just for desensitizing injections, and normally they take prescription and nonprescription drugs besides.

Allergy costs can be high in other ways too. For example, allergists normally encourage young patients to participate as fully as possible in sports. When an athlete's allergies are controlled, he often can compete as effectively as others, doctors say. Allergy-affected athletes have shown this is so. Yet as University of Oklahoma athletic director Wade Walker attests, coaches and others don't see it that way.

"You bet asthma is considered a handicap," Walker declares. "If there were two equally skillful athletes, one with and one without asthma, there's no question we would choose the one without it. It's a pity, in a way. The asthmatic kid works so hard to gain competence and endurance. But that's the way it is."

An allergy is a bizarre bodily reaction to invading foreign substances, called allergens or antigens. These substances cause most persons little trouble.

When antigens enter a normal person through the nose, say, antibodies protect the body until the alien substance leaves the system. In allergic persons, however, traitorous antibodies ally with the invader to produce histamine, a chemical that causes swelling of mucous membranes and tissue just beneath the skin. It also promotes itchiness and the release of certain fluids. Thus the watery eyes of the hay-fever victim and the swelling in asthmatics of cordlike muscles that wrap parts of the bronchial tree. As those irritated muscles enlarge they strangle equally sore, swollen portions of the bronchial tubes, or windpipes, and forcibly reduce the amount of air the victim can breathe.

Misbehaving antibodies also help make bradykinin, a chemical that causes smooth muscles, such as those in the lung, to contract involuntarily, producing spasms.

Allergens are legion. Among the most infamous:

pollens, molds, feathers, foods, man-made chemicals, the venom of bees and other stinging insects, animal dandruff, and dust or, as some allergists think, microscopic mites that ride along on dust motes. Mites are insects that under the microscope look like tiny crabs.

Allergens infiltrate the ears, nose, eyes, and mouth. In defenseless bodies they can cause such things as sinusitis; nose polyps, or growths; dermatitis, or eczema; upset stomach; and hives as well as asthma and hay.fever, which comes from pollens, not hay.

Patients can and frequently do have the symptoms of several diseases at once. A hay-fever patient may put up with steady postnasal drainage, headache, general congestion, stuffed ear passages and thus impaired hearing, as well as with itching and sneezing. The same for asthmatics, who also frequently have sore throats and chest and back pains. Serious allergies can cause nausea not only from food allergy but from constantly flowing mucous.

There are no cures for these symptoms. Occasionally youngsters who have allergies seem to "outgrow" them. But normally the patient must rely on attempts to avoid offending allergens, on medication to reduce symptoms, and on injections, which allergists prefer to call desensitization or hyposensitization therapy. Taken together, these measures can aid most patients.

The injections contain small amounts of the substances the patient reacts to. The goal is to gradually increase dosages until, without reacting, the patient can tolerate reasonably high-level exposure to allergens that otherwise would make him ill. Scientists don't yet know how well desensitization works. Some patients seem to profit from it considerably; others don't.

Further, the antihistamines taken to reduce swelling and stop postnasal drippage can cause drowsiness. And ephedrine, a commonly prescribed asthma medication, can cause lethargy, vertigo, headache, diarrhea, and skin eruptions.

Of course, physicians try to prevent such things. Still, the combination of symptoms and drug reactions often are sufficient to make patients unusually tired, irritable, moody, and seemingly disinterested at work or school.

Elimination of allergens reduces dependence on shots or drugs. That's one reason why Dr. Barkin and others involved argue so strongly for their Montgomery County, Maryland, school program. Says Barkin:

"Consider what it's like for the allergic child who must work in a schoolroom that's coated with chalk and house dust, stuffed with pets, built with materials that exude allergens, draped with improperly treated fabrics, sprayed with reaction-causing insecticides, swept with sawdust, and that reeks with lab-chemical odors.

"The kid can't escape. He fights his reactions, but the atmosphere takes its toll. 'Attention-fatigue' syndrome sets in, which means that the child's body tires and his ability to concentrate wanes."

Mrs. Frances Duncan, president of the Metropolitan Washington (D.C.) Chapter of the Allergy Foundation of America, is the prime mover in establishing the new "allergy plan." She relates: "We parents nurse the children. We see them get worse at times just from going to school, and we've come to believe that the schools frequently counter all efforts at therapy. We think our youngsters are being handicapped in learning. We don't want our children singled out as 'different' or have them embarrassed or coddled. That's why we developed 'the plan.' It will make things uniformly better.

Richard E. Wagner, Ph.D., the school system's assistant superintendent of instructional services, anticipates little trouble implementing the program. Besides providing school staffs with instruction about allergies, it includes such basics as utilizing mold-repressing paints; switching to less-odorous cleaning products; keeping floors clean, rugs vacuumed, and air-duct filters clean; and notifying parents of impending major maintenance work such as painting and construction. The notification allows parents to keep children home on the theory that one or two days of deliberate absence will amount to less than the time lost should fumes and dusts trigger an allergy flare-up.

Also as part of the program, Elizabeth A. D. Mattern, M.D., chairman of the school system's medical-advisory committee, is arranging for all school nurses to receive detailed, up-to-date briefings on allergies and their effects.

The Government's push on allergy began just three years ago when the Department of Health, Education, and Welfare's National Institute of Allergy and Infectious Diseases (NIAID) started giving grants and establishing allergy "centers" around the nation. This was the first effort of its kind since a chronicler first recorded the allergy-reaction phenomenon after Egyptian king Menes' death from a hornet sting in 2641 B.C.

One reason for the delay, says Charles H. Kirkpatrick, a ranking NIAID clinician and researcher, is that "the public has had a skewed interpretation of what a 'significant' disease is, and investing dollars in 'insignificant' allergy research hasn't been a popular notion.

"But if you agree that a significant disease is one that affects the victim's life significantly, then allergies are significant. I have a truck-driver patient who needs antihistamines but is so affected by them he can't drive.

And there's a lawyer patient who was ruining his practice by continually cancelling appointments. He had nocturnal asthma, couldn't sleep, and he couldn't function in daytime without sleep. Those things are 'significant.'"

Officials who allocate research dollars now think so too. They added more research centers to the 14 already set up to seek methods of preventing and better treating allergies. Research is "fast-moving" and the public will see "clinical gains" within two or three years, predicts one NIAID official.

But there have been gains already. Scientists have reported, for example, that asthmatics—who frequently take aspirin to relieve allergy-caused chest pains—have a greater incidence of adverse reaction to aspirin than normal persons. Aspirin can precipitate bronchospasms in asthmatics. Dr. Richard Lockey, an Air Force physician and one of several doctors studying aspirin allergy, says asthmatics should avoid aspirin and ask their doctor's advice about an aspirin substitute to use instead.

Another study established that toddlers who receive anesthesia have a greater incidence of respiratory allergies than others. "It's just another argument against elective surgery for young people," says Dr. Douglas Johnstone, one of the three University of Rochester medical investigators who made the finding.

And research by Dr. Hyman Chai and four others from the National Asthma Center in Denver belies the widely held assumption that psychological factors cause asthma and other allergic diseases. Chai explains: "It's not true. We have shown that emotions play a part, as they do in all diseases. Emotions can trigger an asthmatic attack. But a fouled-up psyche doesn't initiate the disease."

Chai insists the distinction is important. "Once laymen decide that asthma or allergy is 'simply emotional,' they tend to judge that the victim's family should straighten its morals or some such thing. People unrealistically decide that the allergy patient isn't sick. That's no good."

Indeed. It's just that misconception that has caused so much extra distress for allergy victims.

Vasectomies
May Cause Problems

A vasectomy has become a status symbol in certain sets, a topic of cocktail-party conversation. Men who have undergone the sterilization operation sometimes sport a vasectomy pin: the traditional male symbol with a gap in the circle. Now vasectomy advocates see another gap in their future—a confidence gap.

Vasectomies go back to the late Nineteenth Century. But only since 1970 have they become one of the most common operations in the United States, and the surgery most frequently performed on U.S. adult males.

This upsurge delights population-control proponents, who see vasectomy as a simple, relatively inexpensive, safe, and almost foolproof means of birth control. Indeed, some sound like evangelists as they preach their gospel of vasectomies.

But amid the torrent of glad tidings are widening eddies of mild concern about some philosophical aspects and even the safety of vasectomies.

A vasectomy can be performed in a doctor's office under local anesthesia. Short sections of the *vas deferens*, the two sperm-carrying tubes in the scrotum, are snipped out and the tubes are tied off. The body continues to produce sperm, but none can be ejaculated.

Although the operation takes only 15 or 20 minutes, it is not painless. "There is discomfort," acknowledges one surgeon, "a feeling of being kicked by a mule. But this lasts for only a day or two."

Nor is a vasectomy always problem-free. "A small number of patients have minor complications with minimal disability," says Dr. Harold Lear of Mount Sinai medical school in New York City. These include swelling, infection and minor bleeding. In rare cases cysts and knots of scar tissue develop, or the blood supply to a testicle is blocked and it atrophies.

Still, vasectomies appear safer, less painful, and cheaper than female sterilizations, which require hospitalization and abdominal surgery. An outpatient vasectomy generally costs $100 to $200. This, coupled with concern about population problems and the changing male attitude about who should bear responsibility for birth control, partly explains the operation's increasing popularity.

No one knows precisely how many vasectomies have been performed in the United States in the last decade, but the Association for Voluntary Sterilization (AVS) puts the number at around three million. The increase in recent years has been sharp.

Lea, Inc., a company that gathers and publishes medical statistics, reports that private physicians performed 200,000 vasectomies in 1969, 699,000 in 1970, and 714,000 in 1971. Lea's figures do not include vasectomies by military doctors, at state institutions, or at public clinics such as those run by the Planned Parenthood Federation of America.

Frequently the 1972 vasectomy estimate runs to one million, which would place it second in number only to tonsillectomies among U.S. operations. That figure, however, may be extremely high. Lea found that private physicians performed 400,000 vasectomies in the first six months of 1971 and only 298,000 in the like period of 1972.

Part of the great leap upward in vasectomies in 1970 resulted from fears raised by medical reports of side effects of birth-control pills. And the lesson of the Pill has not been lost on some medical men, who wonder if history will repeat itself. They note that the Pill was prescribed widely for over a decade before its side effects were generally recognized. And they wonder if some unknown danger lurks in vasectomies.

"My own impression is that when all the data are in, the vasectomy will prove to be a harmless procedure," says Mount Sinai's Lear. "But you just don't operate on a million men a year without looking for effects. You don't just rely on impressions."

The hunt for adverse effects is on, both here and abroad. The National Institute of Child Health and Human Development, for example, has awarded 10 contracts totaling $925,889 to investigate the long-term medical effects of vasectomies.

What has sparked much of this concern are reports by Dr. H. J. Roberts of the Palm Beach Institute for Medical Research—a private, nonprofit organization in Florida —and Dr. John B. Henry of the State University of New York's Upstate Medical Center in Syracuse.

Roberts reports finding a number of men who developed serious medical problems—including multiple sclerosis, recurring infections, blood-clotting difficulties, rheumatoid arthritis, lung problems, and mental disorders—after their vasectomies.

His findings and their implications are extremely controversial. Dr. Joseph Davis, professor of urology at New York Medical College and president of AVS, calls Roberts' work "an unscientific study." He says Roberts has proved no cause-and-effect relationship, but has shown only that some men who had vasectomies later developed serious medical problems. This, he says, could be pure coincidence.

Henry's report disturbs medical men more; at AVS it is known as the "Henry Scare." Henry and Dr. Young Ja Choi, now at Bronx Lebanon Hospital in New York City, found antibodies that can damage some body cells in 9 of the 12 vasectomy patients they examined.

In theory the body absorbs the sperm produced after a vasectomy. The Henry-Choi report raised the possibility that the body produces antibodies to fight the sperm, just as antibodies often destroy transplanted hearts. If so, this might scramble the immunity system and increase a man's susceptibility to some ailments.

But no one knows whether the antibodies portend future trouble for vasectomy patients. "We detected some antibody, but that is all we can say at this point," says Choi. "I don't think people have to worry about their vasectomies at this point."

The new popularity of vasectomy also has raised questions of whether it should be performed on all who want it.

"The medical profession should not condone vasectomy 'on demand' any more than it would tolerate any other biological mutilation 'on demand,'" Dr. Lear wrote in an editorial in the Journal of the American Medical Association in 1972.

He argues that perhaps 3 per cent of the men who seek a vasectomy want it subconsciously to punish their wives or as an act of self-castration. "If a patient came and wanted a finger cut off, a doctor would at least ask why," says Lear, "I don't think vasectomies should be any different. If a patient is looking for the resolution of an emotional problem, he is not going to find it in a vasectomy."

Doctors agree it is best if the wife fully approves of her husband's decision. "We know if a husband and wife don't agree, the chances of problems [between them] are much greater than if both agree," says Lear.

Some question whether patients are being adequately informed about the permanency of a vasectomy. Only 15 to 25 per cent of the attempts to reverse the operation succeed, so a man must consider his operation permanent.

Yet a survey for the National Institute of Child Health and Human Development found that 18 per cent of the men who had vasectomies, or their wives, thought the operation could easily be reversed.

For years population-control advocates urged wider use of vasectomies. They were delighted when so many men complied. And now they hope nothing will happen, such as adverse medical side effects, to spoil their crusade.

Checking-up on Physicians

AN angry Illinois doctor proposes a new TV series, *Marcus Welby Chained*. It would dramatize how the Government will "force" physicians to give patients "cheap, skimpy" medical care under a new Federal program called Professional Standards Review Organizations (PSROs), says Dr. James Turner of Elmhurst, Ill. One TV episode, says Turner, should focus on Dr. Thomas Hayes of North Andover, Mass., who quit his medical practice because of PSROs. Declares the unhappy Hayes:

"A doctor will have to practice mediocre medicine under PSROs, or he'll be in trouble. No doctor's records will be confidential. Even if I'm treating a drug-abuse patient, Federal people can walk in, flash a badge, and force me to hand over his records."

Strong stuff. But is it true? Will this controversial program of peer review, in which doctors check up on other doctors to make sure they give quality medical care, actually produce mediocre care? Will it invade the privacy of the doctor-patient relationship?

Not at all, says Dr. Henry Simmons, the Government official in charge of setting up PSROs. Simmons asserts that PSROs will help patients by educating doctors on better treatment methods, by uncovering practices "outside the scope of good medicine," and by rapidly bringing "appropriate innovations" into medicine. He insists the confidentiality of patients' records will remain secure. And he's confident that PSROs will achieve their goal of improving health care by checking to see if care is medically necessary, of professional quality, and given in the right health facility.

Unlike Turner and Hayes, many doctors support this kind of peer review. For instance, 950 of Utah's 1,400 licensed physicians signed cards indicating willingness to take part in a peer-review program that's a prototype of PSROs.

The concept generates sharp disagreement, yet nearly everyone agrees that PSROs will have a significant impact on America's health-care system. Together with such proposals as national health insurance and health-maintenance organizations, it's clear that with PSROs the nation is on the verge of a "rare and remarkable" advance in health care, Simmons says.

"Some would say that we are in the midst of the most significant change in the public-private health partnership since the adoption of Medicare and Medicaid some eight years ago," says Simmons. "Frankly, I think that understates the case."

President Nixon, in his health message to Congress in 1974, proposed a comprehensive health-insurance plan. He said PSROs would be an important part of it, "charged with maintaining high standards of care and reducing needless hospitalization."

Under PSROs—a few were to begin operation in 1974 —doctors will check nearby doctors' performance under rules outlined broadly in Federal law but filled in with specific details by local physicians. Medical peer review has existed in various forms for many years, but with spotty effectiveness. Some hospitals run effective peer reviews of surgical procedures, admissions, length of stay, and deaths; others don't. Peer review of patients treated in doctors' offices—which may evolve under PSROs—has been rare.

The PSRO concept originated with foundations for medical care, "group practices without walls," in which doctors affiliate loosely to provide comprehensive health services to such groups as Federal employes or teacers. A "third-party payer"—such as an insurance company or the Government—also is involved.

The first foundation, established in 1954 in San Joaquin County, California, found that claims-payment decisions often involved issues of quality of medical care. Had the doctor given appropriate treatment? If not, should he be paid? Doctors began checking up on their colleagues. "The approach was at once novel and effective. A provider of health services does not dismiss lightly the genteel disagreement of his colleagues," says the American Association of Foundations of Medical Care.

Prior to foundations, most peer review was conducted after the illness. The foundations—more than 60 now exist—emphasize peer review throughout the illness' course. This approach interested Sen. Wallace Bennett, Utah Republican and ranking minority member of the Senate Finance Committee. The committee was puzzled in the late 1960s over what to do about soaring costs of Medicare and Medicaid, the Government's health programs for the aged and poor, respectively.

Says a committee report: "The costs of the Medicare hospital-insurance program will overrun estimates made in 1967 by some $240 billion over a 35-year period. Medicaid costs are also rising at precipitous rates."

Two factors accounted for the startling increases. Costs of hospital rooms, surgical procedures, and doctor's visits rose. So did the *number* of health services pro-

71

vided to the aged and poor. Witnesses told the committee that a significant proportion of these services "are probably not medically necessary."

Convinced that unnecessary services were being given by doctors and paid for by taxpayers, Bennett introduced amendments to the Social Security Act to establish PSROs patterned somewhat after foundations. His amendments passed Congress in 1972. Now, after some early management fumbling in the Department of Health, Education, and Welfare (HEW), the law is being implemented under Simmons' crisp leadership.

HEW has designated 203 PSRO areas nationally. Sparsely populated states such as Utah will have one PSRO; more-populous states will have several. In each area a doctors' group is expected to apply to HEW to become the official PSRO. This could be a foundation, a medical society, or an *ad hoc* group. If no group responds by Jan. 1, 1976, the HEW Secretary will designate an organization, such as a local health department, as the PSRO.

Each PSRO will set its own criteria of quality of care. Guidance will be available from national medical-specialty associations. To admit an appendectomy patient to a hospital, for instance, should all three classic symptoms—right-side pain, high white-cell count, and nausea be present, or are two enough? How long should he be hospitalized? What medication should he receive? X-rays?

At first PSROs will concentrate on hospital care, later extending to nursing homes and mental hospitals. A PSRO may petition the HEW Secretary to apply peer review to treatment in doctors' offices. That, if it happens, will bring hot protests from some doctors.

The PSRO law applies to patients whose bills are

paid by Government programs: Medicare, Medicaid, and maternal-health and child welfare. Says Simmons: "Initially the program will have an impact on over 300,000 physicians, several hundred thousand other health professionals, 11 million hospital discharges, and 50 million people who are eligible for Medicare and Medicaid . . ."

If a doctor modifies his treatment methods for Medicare and Medicaid patients because of PSRO, he's likely to modify them for all patients. So all patients will be affected at least indirectly.

Though PSROs' operations will vary, the Utah peer-review program gives an idea of how one might work. The Utah Professional Review Organization (UPRO) was established in July 1972 as a nonprofit foundation of the Utah State Medical Association. Says Dr. Alan Nelson, a Salt Lake City internist and UPRO's president: "The physicians in Utah recognized there had to be some kind of public accountability for quality health care and cost containment. Otherwise, we felt some bureaucratic decision would be forced on us from the outside."

UPRO functions in five hospitals—three in Salt Lake City and two in Ogden—and covers one-fourth of Utah's population, including 120,000 Federal employes, 70,000 school employes, and 80,000 Medicaid and neighborhood-health-center patients. Twelve commerical insurers are negotiating with UPRO for coverage.

UPRO patients come under review while in the hospital. In each hospital a registered nurse, called a nurse co-ordinator, keeps tabs on each patient covered by UPRO—an average of 75 patients daily. She prepares a profile on each patient, listing details on admission, therapy, X rays and other tests, diagnosis, and treatment. She matches what is being done against what should be done under criteria for care developed by leading Utah specialists.

If she finds something amiss, she informs the doctor who is UPRO's medical adviser in the hospital. That happened recently when a patient was admitted with phlebitis, inflammation of a vein. His symptoms indicated a pulmonary embolism, but his physician had failed to order a chest X ray or an electrocardiogram.

Says Susan Beye, who trains nurse co-ordinators: "The nurse co-ordinator talked to the medical adviser, and he in turn talked to the doctor. The doctor was irate, but the next day we had the chest film that confirmed the suspected problem."

Doctors usually resolve the issue among themselves in an informal, educational way. The key to success, says David Buchanan, UPRO executive director, is to "gently coax [them] into line, not to beat them over the head with their mistakes."

Occasionally a doctor won't be coaxed, and UPRO withdraws "certification" in the case; the insurer doesn't have to pay for the patient's hospital care from that moment on. That happened 24 times in the 20,000 cases reviewed in UPRO's first 18 months.

When certification was withdrawn, the hospital had to arrange with the patient either to leave or pay his own bill. The patient and hospital officials couldn't have been happy with the stubborn doctors.

Results and findings of UPRO:

● The length of stay in hospitals dropped more than one-third of a day per UPRO patient.

● Hospital charts are better-documented because physicians are filling in information they left out before.

● Half the doctors were failing to take a history of previous bleeding before doing a tonsillectomy. UPRO wrote all doctors that this was critical to quality care; a patient with a bleeding problem could bleed to death during a tonsillectomy.

● Many doctors failed to check for tenderness in a patient's legs after an apparent heart attack. A blood clot that has traveled from calf to lung can simulate a heart attack; tender legs indicate a clot.

UPRO is likely to become the official PSRO for Utah, and though some doctors grumble about the program, most share the view of Dr. Burtis Evans, a Salt Lake City internist: "If properly handled, I think this program will be of great benefit to us all. It is possible for any doctor to drift into bad habits. I would much prefer one of my colleagues pointing them out to me than to have some Government official do it. Doctors should not be afraid of criticism, and when they are shown to be wrong they should change their ways."

And if they won't change? That's a sensitive question, because the PSRO amendments say a doctor may be liable for up to $5,000 of a patient's medical bills if he can't justify treatment that falls outside the range of norms specificied by his PSRO. The doctor, however, may request advance PSRO approval for an extended or costly treatment or an elective hospital admission. If the PSRO board turns him down he can ask for reconsideration. Then he can appeal to a state-wide council and, finally, to the HEW Secretary.

Another sensitive issue is computerizing records of patients, doctors, and hospitals. This worries Dr. Claude Welch of Boston, who heads the Guidelines of Care task force of the American Medical Association (AMA) and is president of the American College of Surgeons. He writes in the New England Journal of Medicine, "The agencies that control the computers could control the practice of medicine."

In an interview, Welch says he also worries about possible public access to "profiles" of patients, doctors, and hospitals that will be created by PSROs. "Information leaks could occur and damage certain people," says Welch. "Doctors worry about that almost more than anything else. A minor peccadillo could be recorded and turn up in the future."

HEW officials insist that the profiles will remain confidential unless a doctor wants to make his profile public, perhaps in court to defend himself against a malpractice suit. That's fine for doctors, but what about patients? How can they know if a doctor is practicing poor or dangerous medicine?

Apparently they can't know, except by word of mouth. PSROs will be run by doctors, though laymen may be on advisory boards. The names of erring doctors aren't likely to be made public.

Limitation on participation in PSROs has drawn the ire of the Health Research Group, affiliated with Ralph Nader. Robert McGarrah of the group says PSROs should include doctors from outside the PSRO area to minimize "back-scratching."

Leda Judd of the National Urban Coalition, who with McGarrah and Patricia Kenney wrote a report critical of PSROs, says that some nonphysicians should be on peer-review panels. "Why are doctors so afraid of letting others see what they've done?" she asks. "It's not that I want to watch a doctor operate. There are a variety of health elements that a layman can help assess, such as hours of medical service and billings in hospitals."

Also sharply critical of PSROs, though from a different viewpoint, is the Association of American Physicians and Surgeons, which represents several thousand physicians. It has filed a Federal suit asking that the PSRO law be declared unconstitutional because, among other reasons, it interferes with the doctor-patient relationship.

The huge AMA has vacillated on PSROs, at various times opposing, going along with, and helping to implement the peer-review system. The AMA's present stand, which it tried to clarify after its December 1973 convention supported both repeal and amendment of the law, seems to be to help set up PSROs and simultaneously seek amendments to weaken the program's impact on doctors.

The most vital issue in the PSRO debate is of course the quality of medical care. The whole point of PSROs is to upgrade quality, and many doctors think that will happen. Yet physicians such as Thomas Hayes of Massachusetts think the opposite will result.

"If I'm harassed in my medical practice by a third party," he says, meaning the PSROs, "I may make some bad decisions. What will happen to the patient who is sent home from the hospital too soon because PSRO tells me how long he can stay? I'm too busy to go to Boston to the PSRO and plead for longer care."

Hayes couldn't tolerate this prospect. He sent letters to his patients saying he was closing his practice after 19 years. He'll support his wife and their seven children at home—three more are grown—by working in hospital emergency rooms or in industrial medicine. where PSRO rules will affect him much less.

When his patients asked him to reconsider, Hayes replied, "If you keep politicians out of the practice of medicine, I'll come back."

Another PSRO casualty is Dr. George Nash of

Tucson, Ariz., who wrote to the AMA's American Medical News saying he had read of Hayes' retirement and would retire too. At 43 Nash was at his peak as a neurosurgeon. He had the largest neurological practice in Arizona, was president-elect of the state neurological society, and was a board member of the state medical society.

Nash sees PSROs as the final, intolerable intrusion of Government into medicine. He says he will write a book, perhaps enter an Episcopal seminary, and maybe practice medicine eventually in another country.

Firmly and sadly he declares: "I will never practice medicine again in the United States of America."

Are Useful Drugs Banned?

AN Italian wrote an American doctor seeking help. He planned to visit the United States with an epileptic daughter, whose malady is controllable only by a drug called Depakine. The father asked whether someone in the United States could supply the drug. He was advised to bring along all the Depakine his daughter needs because there is no way he can get it legally in the United States.

That's one father's solvable problem. But what of the many epileptics in this country who might obtain deliverance from their awful spasms with Depakine? They'll have to wait until the drug is either approved here, which may be never, or they can use another, perhaps less-effective drug.

Indeed, the American drug industry and some prominent physicians, scientists, and editorialists charge that the United States is forfeiting pre-eminence in drug development to Europe. Some contend that Europeans are using safe, effective drugs not available to Americans. They call it a "therapy gap," and they attribute it to the strict drug-development laws enforced by the U.S. Food and Drug Administration (FDA).

"There is no therapy gap," says Dr. Henry Simmons, former director of the FDA's Bureau of Drugs. "There is no known, safe, and efficacious drug in the world for which no counterpart is available here."

Yet consider a study made by a West German pharm-

79

aceutical company: The United States in 1961 discovered 31 new drugs, 11 were discovered in West Germany, and 9 were discovered in France; in 1970 the U.S. share of new drugs had fallen to 5, West Germany's was 7, and France's was 21. The tough new drug-control laws were enacted in 1962.

Dr. Robert D. Dripps, before his death the vice president for medical affairs at the University of Pennsylvania, said the U.S. regulatory system chokes off creative drug research and "may be depriving the practicing physician of agents beneficial to patient care."

Dr. Dripps spoke for 21 concerned medical scientists known as the Dripps Committee, which included one Nobel laureate, four winners of the Albert Lasker Award, and the deans of several medical schools. In a letter to a congressman known to be critical of the FDA, Dripps said, "Doctors are limited in the drugs they can use to help the severe arthritic, the psychotic, the patient with cancer, stroke, or coronary heart disease."

The possibility of a therapy gap seems strongest in the treatment of a few specific medical problems, such as high blood pressure. Hypertension experts are upset because at least four antihypertension drugs aren't available in this country. But interviews with observers of the drug market, with drug researchers at the National Institutes of Health (NIH), in academic medicine, and with representatives of the drug industry do not support the implication that a Government agency is causing needless suffering for many Americans. Neither did 1973 testimony at a hearing on drug development conducted by Democratic Sen. Gaylord Nelson of Wisconsin.

It is "not true" to say that people are being "deprived" of new drugs, says Paul de Haen, whose company annually reviews more than 12,000 drug reports and publishes an analysis of new drugs introduced throughout the world. In his "Annual Review of New Drugs" for 1971, de Haen said the new drugs developed in the seven countries surveyed offer little "real innovation" in therapy or permit treatment of diseases previously not responding to drug therapy. "With the use of these drugs," said de Haen, "the physician will be able to vary and refine the treatment of his patients and bring relief perhaps more rapidly or with less side effects."

Appearing before an FDA drug advisory committee on the question of European versus American drugs, Dr. Dripps acknowledged that "none of us [on the Dripps Committee] knows with certainty what contribution any of these new [European] drugs is making to the health of patients."

Dr. John Moxley, former member of that advisory committee and dean of the University of Maryland Medical School, feels Dripps failed to prove the United States is falling behind Europe. Moxley said that "the FDA is doing a pretty good job of charting a very, very rocky course."

Most analysts of the drug market concede a numerical drop in American drug development, but they point out that the drug laws have not affected the discovery of "important" therapeutic advances," drugs that treat diseases for which no previous help existed. The law has slowed improvements in some existing drugs—improvements that are sometimes trivial and sometimes significant.

Moreover the frustration of not being able to use a drug to free patients from the purgatory of cancer, mental illness, heart disease, and the like is attributable more to ignorance of what causes these problems than to drug regulations. Pharmacologists are fond of saying the discovery of antibiotics and tranquilizers was "easy" compared with the riddles posed by the degenerative diseases.

However, drug researchers say there are drugs available elsewhere that should be introduced to the U.S. market. The drugs, which control certain types of epilepsy, diabetes, hypertension, asthma, rheumatism, and cholesterol levels, don't offer help where none previously existed, but the researchers feel the European drugs do the job faster or more effectively. They do not agree on whether the delay of these drugs is reason to relax the drug laws.

Dr. Donald S. Frederickson of the National Heart and Lung Institute wants a long-delayed ruling from the FDA on an anticholesterol drug called cholestyramine, but he's willing to wait for it. "The safety of the patient is paramount," says Fredrickson, and he prefers that the FDA "err on the side of greater discretion and care."

But Dr. John Laragh, a medical professor at Columbia University and former head of the Hypertension Council of the American Heart Association, is disappointed by the FDA's holding up of four antihypertension drugs. Laragh says 25 million Americans have high blood pressure, which has been associated with stroke, heart failure, kidney failure, and coronary thrombosis.

Laragh and others say the FDA insists on an unrealistically high margin of safety and thus delays and kills many good drugs. "There is no such thing as risk-free," says Laragh.

Still others blame the public. Dr. Sheldon G. Gilgore, president of Pfizer Pharmaceuticals, says a growing societal attitude clearly implies that the only risk now acceptable is "no risk at all." Henry W. Gadsen, chairman of Merck & Co., Inc., says: "Carried to its ultimate, the consumer view is that no risk is acceptable and that perfection is the only level of performance to be tolerated."

But Henry Simmons says, "Society feels this safeguard is justified." He says the FDA has protected Americans from several drug-related epidemics that occurred elsewhere.

In 1966 asthma killed 7 per cent of the children between the ages of 10 and 14 who died in England and Wales. Asthma deaths rose also in Scotland, Ireland, New Zealand, and Australia, but not in the United States. Investigators, who traced the deaths to a drug used to help asthmatics breathe, said the concentration of the drug in those countries was five times greater than that licensed in the United States. Great Britain is often cited as one of the countries moving ahead of us in drug development.

The FDA's successes do not deter its critics, who argue that the regulations may save asthmatics, but they also delay or cause the loss of a drug that might save the lives of a greater number of persons suffering from other ailments.

Dr. J. Richard Crout, director of the FDA's Bureau of Drugs, is the individual most responsible for deciding which drugs reach the market. He was asked how much drug risk the FDA allows the public to take and how the agency makes that decision.

"When we think of protecting the consumer," Crout said, "the protection very much includes a sensitivity to the seriousness of the disease being treated." He said that among other things the FDA considers the number of people who would benefit from the drug and the availability of alternative drugs on the market.

For instance, the agency licensed an extremely powerful and dangerous anticancer drug called methotrexate because cancer patients have few other choices. To treat a neurological disease that kills every child who gets it, researchers at the National Institute of Neurological Disease and Stroke are permitted by FDA to use a powerful drug that may injure healthy cell tissue.

The agency disappointed some safety-oriented critics by approving oral contraceptive drugs, which it deemed the most effective type of contraceptive available, despite a statistical association between use of the oral contraceptives and thromboembolism (blockage of blood flow) and evidence the drugs may cause cancer, impair liver function, and cause abnormal genital bleeding. On the other hand, says Dr. Crout, the FDA probably wouldn't license a dangerous tranquilizer because other relatively safe and effective tranquilizers are available.

Profit considerations may also suppress drug development as effectively as drug laws. No drugs exist to control the forms of epilepsy that afflict about half of the country's four million epileptics. But that potential market of two million epileptics doesn't appear to be attractive to drug companies. To stimulate the profit motive, Dr. J. Kiffin Penry, chief of epilepsy research at NIH, has actually supplied drug companies with market data to prove they can make money on epilepsy. "It's what has to be done," says Penry. "If the boss thinks one drug is more profitable than another, he goes with it."

FDA officials concede that both the drug law and the manner in which they enforce it have slowed the development of new drugs, which on the average, the drug industry says, takes seven years to develop at a cost of $7 million. The 1962 law requires that drug developers prove a drug's "efficacy": They must show that the drug does what they claim it will do, and the law spells out precise, time-consuming procedures for proving it. Often the FDA wants to know how a drug will affect special groups, such as children or old people. The tests are expensive, but the agency considers the information worth having.

Dr. Charles C. Edwards, a former FDA commissioner, has conceded that there are "deficiencies in our approach to new-drug applications; there are inequities and delay; bureaucratic hang-ups, and, even as our critics charge, occasional demands for trivial information."

It is difficult to say what has contributed more to the slowdown in drug development—the drug laws, the drug bureaucrats, or our ignorance of why we get sick.

Few question the need for strict testing requirements; studies of the research performed by drug manufacturers before the 1962 amendments to the drug law show that much of it was poorly done. But even the most conscientious industry scientists, who work with their company's drug problems rather than its profit margins, have been frustrated by the FDA's pace.

The drug industry and its regulator have fought bitterly in the past, but a mood of conciliation seems to be developing. Joseph Stetler, president of the Pharmaceutical Manufacturers Association, a trade group, has said that the "FDA, the pharmaceutical industry, and the health professionals of this country now have an opportunity to bring about a truly constructive working relationship . . ."

Those who have rapped the FDA for occasionally acting like protectors of the drug industry get jumpy when a spokesman of the drug industry says something like that. But most independent researchers have had their fill of the drug wars. If some of the European drugs can help Americans safely and effectively, they'd like to see them on the market.

But they don't like the implication that the "therapy gap" is denying help to those afflicted with a wasting cancer or a crippling muscular disease. They want to carry out their efforts against these problems free of the public and political pressure that an issue as highly charged as the therapy gap can create.

"There's a lot of bad blood around," says the FDA's Crout. "That's what we're trying to clear away."

Seeking a Night's Sleep

WHILE doctors debate such esoteric questions as whether sleep is truly necessary, nearly one in every three American adults just wishes for a decent night of it. They suffer from some degree of insomnia, all 45 million of them.

For insomniacs, getting enough sleep can become a desperate struggle. It may mean powerful, addictive sleeping pills, sessions with a psychiatrist, and costly expenditures for such things as new beds, sound machines, humidifiers, and air purifiers. All together, about $2 billion is spent annually in the pursuit of sleep, yet relief is fleeting.

"There is strong evidence that even among people without a situational or medical disturbance in their lives, 80 to 90 per cent of all chronic insomniacs show a psychiatric disorder," says Dr. Anthony Kales, the foremost investigator of insomnia among the growing number of sleep researchers. "Some people say insomnia causes the psychiatric disorder, but we believe that insomnia isn't causative, that it's a symptom."

The primary reason people are emotionally or psychologically unhealthy, and restless sleepers, is shifting. In the 1950s and 1960s, psychiatrists say, they were seeing more people suffering from anxiety and its attendant worries. Now they say more and more people are suffering from depression. Says Leon Marder, a Los Angeles psychiatrist: "Estimates are that there are about 10 million depressed people walking the streets, and a huge number of them have trouble sleeping."

Insomnia is, of course, either the inability to fall asleep at night, periodic reawakenings throughout the night, premature waking at 3 or 4 a.m., or any combination of the three. "There's one thing about insomnia I tell all my patients," says Gerald Jampolsky, a Tiburon, Calif., psychiatrist. "You don't die from it."

There has always been a great fascination with sleep and dreams, and what they both mean and do for us or to us. We're forever reading about them, and it seems strange to learn there is little solid data in the field. Just recently, however, sleep researchers began learning so much from their studies that they now contend they know really very little at all. The new research keeps knocking all of the old ideas out of whack. For instance:

Remember the theory that you'd go insane if you didn't dream? Nonsense. Or the one that held it was not so terribly important how much you slept, but how much quality, or deep, sleep that you got? Again, nonsense. Or even that you dream only during the stage of sleep called REM, the acronym for the rapid-eye-movement stage? Not true. And there really is a serious debate about whether sleep is necessary.

"It is clear that many of our earlier conceptions about sleep are proving to be wrong," says Dr. William Dement, head of the Stanford University sleep disorders clinic and laboratory. "A lot of people, for example, believe that they're piling up poisons in the body that only sleep can handle. But right now it seems sleep is only necessary to reduce sleepiness. We simply don't understand the brain mechanisms that dictate sleep."

Still, doctors allow that they are gleaning significant facts about sleep and how you can get more of it. For example, if you suffer only mildly from insomnia, there are a number of things you can do that may alleviate your problem. Doctors such as Kales, Dement, and Laverne Johnson at the U.S. Navy's Balboa Hospital in San Diego, though often in professional disagreement, speak generally of the same changes insomniacs should make in their behavior:

✔ Regulate your schedule. Many people confuse their biological rhythms, get their body out of synchronization by trying to go to bed one night at 11 p.m., the next night at 3 a.m., then at 10 p.m. It can be as unsettling as the jet lag that comes from cross-country plane rides. Too, the body seems to work on a 90-minute rhythm, so you are likely to be the most susceptible at, say, 11 p.m. and then again at 12:30 a.m.

✔ Exercise can help. You can increase how deeply you sleep through exercise, though doctors caution that if you exhaust yourself you may have even more trouble sleeping. They recommend that the exercise come earlier in the day, counseling that exertion just before bedtime is not as beneficial.

✔ Relax your mind before retiring. Don't get involved in mentally stimulating or disturbing activity late in the evening. For example, don't get involved in the corporate books, family finances, or any other kind of homework. Instead, read a neutral book or watch the television news, which has a relaxing effect because of its unvarying routine and nature.

✔ If you can't sleep, get up. Don't lie in bed longer than perhaps 10 minutes at a stretch. Johnson says the greatest cure for insomnia is to keep people awake, to keep them out of bed until they're ready for sleep.

✔ Your sleeping environment can be important. Flotation or water beds can help some people, firmer beds still others. The darker the room, the easier it is to sleep. Early-morning sun in the face has its effect, so blackout curtains might be in order. Too, distracting and unexpected noise can awaken the insomniac who normally enjoys a much lighter sleep anyway. Chester Pierce, a professor at Harvard University, says the ghetto could be the model of an environment that deprives people of sleep because of its noise and crowding.

Sleeping pills—hypnotics—are of increasing concern. The over-the-counter antihistamines aren't as strong as the barbiturates prescribed by doctors, and these widely advertised sleeping aids can be helpful if you expect to have trouble sleeping for only a night or two. They are of little help for longer periods.

Kales, who was at the University of California at Los Angeles before establishing his sleep clinic at Pennsylvania State University's Hershey, Pa., Medical Center, has been investigating the effect of the most commonly prescribed sleeping pills. He contends that hardly any of them are effective in inducing sleep after a week or two of use. "The effect of prolonged usage of the pills is to create a drug-dependent insomnia and a poorer night's sleep," he says.

He cites the results of a 1973 Los Angeles Metropolitan Area Survey, conducted by UCLA, indicating about one-third of insomniacs are taking drugs. He says another survey of about 50 Beverly Hills doctors showed that about one-half of their insomniac patients had been prescribed pills for one month, about one-third for three months.

Drug-dependent insomniacs have another set of problems. "They suffer severe withdrawal symptoms," explains Kales. He says that drugs reduce the amount of rapid-eye-movement (REM), or dream-stage sleep.

When a person suddenly quits taking the drugs he experiences a "marked increase" in his dreams and nightmares, which creates a psychological dependence.

This becomes a serious dilemma to the doctor when a patient has a medical disturbance that will interfere with his sleep. Often people take the pills because they can't sleep with pain, for example, and if they didn't have insomnia before, they wind up with it because of the drug's effect.

Sleep researchers agree that insomniacs—both those on drugs and those suffering along without them—should see a doctor. "A person should have a doctor's guidance and help when he starts withdrawing from drugs," says Stanford's Dement.

For the chronic insomniac whose plight is not compounded by drugs, doctors contend that a combination of psychotherapy and pharmacological treatment is normally required. "Insomniacs tend to deny their problems and focus on the symptom, their sleeplessness," says Kales. "They nearly all want an exotic, quick cure."

Sleep disorders result from anxiety, depression, tension, neurosis, or poor physical health, adds Johnson. "There is even a question that a sleep disorder is a medical problem. We have no data to say that the loss of sleep is detrimental, other than how it makes a person feel for having less of it then he feels he needs."

Many theories have been advanced as to how insomniacs can get more sleep. In the past 10 years there has been great interest in such things as "electric sleep," in which a tiny electrical current is passed through the sleeper's brain. This method is most popular in Russia and other Communist-bloc countries. "There was a time that we thought it might be a break-through," says Kales, "but studies show that its effects aren't that beneficial."

Too, biofeedback and other relaxation therapies have helped some people, but doctors warn that the therapy can harm a person with a severe psychological or medical problem. It can even make some psychiatrically disturbed persons a lot worse.

A number of people are cashing in on insomnia. Tom Snyder, host of NBC's wee-hours *Tomorrow* show, says projections when the show premiered last October were for two million viewers each evening. "We've been reaching about three million," says Snyder, "and our audience is growing."

Bill Steed's sleep learning center in San Francisco gets about half of its business from people suffering from either anxiety or depression. "They've already been through the psychiatrists," he says. "Good psychology is good common sense. We lead a life of suggestion, and the message on our records gives you a good image of yourself. Depression, after all, is learned feedback from experience. We simply reprogram people to feel good about themselves." His records for a 30-week course cost $469.

One of the leading water-bed marketers has its own in-house sleep expert. That's Dr. Irving London of Innerspace. "Not all water beds are flotation beds," he says, "and it's important to own a flotation bed, which can cut your tossing and turning by at least 25 per cent."

London says that until recent years no one has questioned the sleeping environment. "I suffered from insomnia myself." he says, "hopping back and forth from barbiturates to stimulants." The answer for him was in his sleeping environment, and purchasing all of what he now says is available and possibly helpful would approach what Hershey's Kales would call a "fetish."

London describes some of the accessories that can enhance a sleep environment: the flotation bed, of course; a "white-sound" machine to reduce noise distractions; a cold-air humidifier; an air purifier to remove dust and pollutants; a clock that slowly changes colors and produces a relaxing, hypnotic effect; and blackout curtains. He doesn't recommend them all, but says that each may have its place, depending upon what keeps a person from sleeping.

All of these sleeping aids, even if effective for many people, would have little impact upon people with serious sleep disorders, and many times insomnia indicates those severe problems. Stanford's Dement says that there is "absolutely no relation" between the amount of sleep a person actually gets when studied in the clinic and the severity of his complaint. Too, he says there is no way to determine whether a person has a severe medical problem without long and costly study of his sleep.

Dement says sleep apnea—a condition where a person stops breathing during his sleep because the brain fails to order it—may have been the cause of death for some people taking heavy doses of sleeping pills. At the very least, he says that sleep apnea can put a huge strain on a person's heart and lungs, when he awakens frequently, gasping for air.

The studies at the nation's three leading sleep clinics —Stanford, Hershey, and Dartmouth in New Hampshire —are doing more to knock down previously accepted theories than to prove them out. Some of the more significant investigations are in areas such as just how much sleep is necessary, and the effect of a limited amount of sleep upon a person. "We can reduce a person's time sleeping until he is overwhelmed by exhaustion, but if the reduction is only an hour or two a night, though the person may feel tired, his performance on the job or at school doesn't suffer," says San Diego's Johnson.

Psychiatrist Jampolsky contends that a person suffering from insomnia should forget that a specified period of sleep is a prerequisite to feeling well. "People should sleep when they are ready," he says. "The body is a good manager. It isn't so necessary to place such a great value on sleep."

Yet all sleep researchers and psychiatrists agree that sleep disorders such as insomnia probably are symptoms of a more serious disorder. "Our biggest effort right now," says Kales, "is to educate the general practitioner who is prescribing the drugs." The fear is that the pills now taken by about 10 million people merely camouflage the real disorder, perhaps even making it more severe.

So, despite the debate about whether sleep is necessary, whether so many hours a night are needed, and precisely what function sleep plays, sleep—or lack of it —remains a major problem for millions. There is no easy cure for most people, particularly since researchers have become so dissatisfied with the current batch of sleeping medications. One thing the doctors are convinced of is that the loss of sleep isn't as harmful as generally believed.

Writes Dr. John Stevens in the British Department of Health's Prescriber's Journal: "Those who regularly lose most sleep throughout their lives—seamen, nurses, and doctors—remain resilient, healthy, and hard working, in spite of such losses over long periods."

And if that doesn't hearten the insomniac, it's well to remember that doctors also agree that warm milk or Ovaltine, just as mom knew, does help.

WOMEN'S PURSES often contain medicines dangerous to children, say two pediatricians who interviewed 300 women in a Brooklyn medical clinic. The doctors say children often rummage through purses looking for candy and gum. But in 50 per cent of the purses the researchers checked the kids would have found headache remedies, "nerve pills," Darvon, Librium, vitamins, nitroglycerine, diet pills, saccharin, and contraceptives. The physicians suggested that mothers of small children keep their pills out of their purses.

⌖

FROSTBITE can be prevented or mitigated by heeding some tips from the American Medical Association. Remember below-freezing temperatures aren't necessary for frostbite to occur if the wind is blowing. Dress properly, and avoid overexertion, excessive perspiration, and contact of bare flesh with cold metal. Don't drink alcohol or smoke. The AMA also suggests that companions should watch each other for signs of ears or nose turning white because the victim can't feel frostbite. In first aid for frostbite, don't touch the frozen part, much less massage it or rub it with snow, the AMA warns. Begin rapid rewarming as soon as possible with a hot bath or hot wet towels changed frequently and applied gently. If no fire or hot water is at hand, place the patient in a sleeping bag or cover with coats and blankets. Hot liquids will help raise the body temperature. The AMA recommends prompt medical attention for any frostbite.

⌖

WARNING: The liquid wax dispensed by many automatic car-washing machines can suddenly obscure your vision in the rain. The National Highway Traffic Safety Administration cites reports from motorists whose windshields became nearly opaque as wipers smeared rain and road grime into the coating. It's an unexpected hazard because the wax-covered glass usually appears exceptionally clear in bright sunlight. Motorists are advised to clean both wipers and glass immediately after a wax application. Rub vigorously with a window-cleaning product or a mixture of detergent and alcohol, then rinse away the solution.

⌖

INVALIDS and handicapped people in Birmingham, Ala., get a mark of distinction that may help them escape household fires. Birmingham firemen place reflective stickers on their doors or in the corridors outside their apartments, thereby alerting both firemen and passers-by that those inside might need special attention in case of fire. For information, write Coy Glasgow, Vulcan Life Insurance Co., Fire Fighters Division, Box 1886, Birmingham, Ala. 35201. The company supplies the stickers in Birmingham and plans to promote the idea throughout the 14 states it serves.

⬤

SUN LAMPS can turn a winter pallor into a summer tan, but they can also cause harm unless used properly. The most frequent accidents involve sunburn or damage to eyes. The proper use of a sun lamp is explained in a free Government publication, titled "Sunlamps." Write to Consumer Product Information, Pueblo, Colo. 81009.

⬤

"MINIBIKES—WHAT EVERY PARENT SHOULD KNOW" is a fact sheet parents may wish to read before they allow children to zoom off on a new minibike, according to the National Highway Traffic Safety Administration. The fact sheet suggest precautions parents should take to protect their children and details potential dangers. For example, it says minibikes are noted for poor handling characteristics and should never be used on sidewalks, streets, highways, or any paved area. A free single copy of the booklet may be ordered from Consumer Product Information, Pueblo, Colo., 81009.

⬤

VISITORS sometimes laugh when the Haitian voodoo man sits down at his drums. But they had better not. Both the Department of Health, Education, and Welfare and the New York City Health Department in 1974 warned travelers to Haiti that a few of those goatskin drums might be deadly indeed.

Drums, wineskins, rugs, and any other items made with untanned Haitian goatskin might be contaminated with anthrax spores, which can cause an acute and virulent respiratory and intestinal disorder that is nearly always fatal in animals and often is in humans. The spores can live for 15 or 20 years on a skin and are difficult to kill.

"People should not attempt to sterilize or decontaminate the items themselves," said a spokesman for the New York health department, "and they certainly shouldn't throw the

96

items away. That could spread the contamination."

Such items, he said, should be wrapped securely in a plastic bag, tied tightly or sealed, and taken to the nearest health department.

The first symptom of anthrax is an ugly pimple, or carbuncle, usually on the hands, arms, or neck, because the anthrax organisms usually transfer when the offending item is handled.

EAR PIERCING with inadequately sterilized instruments has been implicated in some cases of viral hepatitis studied by the U.S. Center for Disease Control. In its review of 702 cases of hepatitis reported in Seattle in 1972, the center found 48 women who had no history of exposure to sources of the disease. The center found statistically significant the fact that seven of the women had undergone ear piercing, two of them at the same establishment. Researchers have concluded that piercing instruments transmitted infection from one woman to the next. The center is continuing surveillance for hepatitis spread by ear piercing and has urged physicians and jewelers to use disposable ear-piercing equipment or to effectively sterilize reusable equipment.

HEARING LOSS is discussed in a new pamphlet from the Council of Better Business Bureaus. "Facts About Hearing Aids" discusses signs of hearing loss and types of deafness and recommends what to do about it. For a single, free copy, send a request for publication 03-250, with a self-addressed, stamped, long envelope to the council, 1150 17th St., N.W., Washington, D.C. 20036.

MORE than half the people of the United States don't eat nutritionally correct meals, says the Department of Agriculture. For those with adequate income it's often apathy or lack of knowledge that stands in the way of good nutrition. So the Government and representatives of the food industry have cooperated to produce an informative 32-page booklet on nutrition. "Food is More than Just Something to Eat" explains how diet at any age can affect the length and quality of one's life. For example, experts say what a young girl eats now is likely to affect the kind of pregnancy she will have years later. The booklet tells what foods are the best sources of various nutrients and how to combine them into a healthful diet. To get a free copy, write Nutrition, Pueblo, Colo. 81009.

◇◦◦◇

PARENTS of children with disabilities may be interested in the Exceptional Parent, a magazine that attempts to provide information for both parents and the professionals who work with their children. The bimonthly magazine deals with problems such as mental retardation, emotional disturbance, chronic illness, and physical, perceptual, and learning disabilities. A subscription costs $10 a year. For more information or for a reprint of "Let Us All Stop Blaming the Parents," and editorial that appeared in the magazine, write the Exceptional Parent, Box 101, Back Bay Annex, Boston 02117.

◇◦◦◇

OLDER PERSONS who keep active and in touch with other people age most successfully, says health experts. But a recent study by American University in Washington, D.C., shows that families too often have no idea what services are available to help the elderly broaden their horizons. In "After 65: Resources for Self-Reliance," Theodore Irwin describes programs such as senior-citizen centers; job opportunities; cultural outlets; day centers; legal and homemaker-health assistance; telephone reassurance; and meal, transportation, visitor, and visiting-nurse services. The new 28-page pamphlet is 35 cents from the Public Affairs Committee, 381 Park Ave. South, New York City 10016.

◇◦◦◇

DENTAL PATIENTS in Pennsylvania can charge their dental work under a new credit plan set up by a bank and the Odontological Society of Western Pennsylvania. Patients are expected to benefit because they'll be less likely to put off essential dental work for financial reasons. Dentists laud reduced bookkeeping chores. Currently the plan is limited to patients of some 1,200 dentists who belong to the society.

◇◦◦◇

HEART PATIENTS who suffer from disease of the coronary arteries should beware of traveling in heavy traffic. A study shows carbon monoxide inhaled on freeways during rush hours is enough to be a serious health hazard to persons with a

98

limited blood flow and oxygen supply to the heart because the gas takes vital space in the blood's oxygen-carrying system. The study, by the Veterans Administration, found that closing car windows and operating the air conditioner offers little protection during dense traffic.

DOWNHILL SKIING is not exercise, contends Dr. Lewis J. Krakauer, a University of Oregon internist. In contrast to cross-country skiing, downhill skiing does little to help muscle endurance or increase cardiac conditioning, he says. Indeed, he believes that stresses from excitement, cold, high altitude, and overdressing may be harmful to a poorly conditioned heart. At a conference on skiing injuries, Krakauer recommended that middle-aged men get heart tests before skiing, then condition themselves by jogging, running, or swimming.

KILLING PAIN in the past usually has meant reliance on drugs that affect a person's entire system, such as anesthetic gases used during operations. Now researchers at the University of Texas Health Science Center at Dallas are working on techniques that focus on specific parts of the body. One method involves use of electronic stimulation of nerves to locate precise sites for injecting a deadening drug. Another uses controlled electrical current through strategically implanted electrodes. University physicians also are studying the results of acupuncture, using fine hypodermic needles instead of traditional Oriental needles. The anesthesiologists report good symptomatic relief for 60 per cent of their acupuncture patients, no relief whatsoever for another 20 per cent, and mixed relief for 20 per cent.

Truth in Packaging Furniture

"TRUTH-IN-PACKAGING" has come to furniture.

All furniture advertised and sold in this country must comply with new Federal Trade Commission (FTC) guidelines designed to help consumers figure out what the items are really made of.

The guidelines provide for disclosure of the use of plastic, vinyl, marble dust, wood veneers, and other materials that simulate solid wood, leather, marble, slate, or any other natural materials. The guidelines also call for fuller disclosure of the composition of upholstery fabrics and stuffings.

What this means is that you won't have to wonder any longer whether that walnut-appearing bookcase is really solid walnut or, instead, pine with a walnut veneer. You'll have to be told that an armchair having the look of leather but bearing a trade name such as "Durahyde" is actually "simulated leather" or "fabric-backed vinyl." And if that couch you're considering buying is stuffed with both latex foam rubber and nonlatex foam and is covered with a fabric made of both nylon and other fibers, any description will have to make those facts clear.

The new rule of thumb for manufacturers and retailers, according to an FTC lawyer, is that "whenever a technique is used that gives a piece of furniture the appearance of being something it's not, the consumer must be told." The guidelines are needed, the lawyer says, because of "widespread misleading advertising and other deceptive practices" in the furniture industry related to the growing use of new techniques and materials.

One of the practices forbidden by the guidelines is representing a piece of furniture made in the United States as being of Danish, Spanish, or other foreign origin. Such furniture should be described in terms such as "Danish style" or "Italian design," the guidelines say. Exceptions are made for some terms such as "French Provincial," "Chinese Chippendale," and "Mediterranean," which the FTC says are considered to have their own identities as a style of furniture.

The guidelines also forbid furniture from being sold as a "floor sample" or "demonstration piece" if it is actually rental or repossessed furniture. Furniture may not be described as "discontinued" unless the manufacturer has stopped making the model or the retailer is selling out his entire stock.

The new disclosures must appear both in advertising and on tags or labels attached to the furniture.

Spotting Turquoise Substitutes

I don't call it turquoise," said Indian-trader Harold Street in Santa Fe, N.M., displaying an attractive piece of jewelry. He pointed to a blue matrix-lined stone within the delicate silverwork of a string-tie holder.

The stone was what is known in the Southwest as "treated" turquoise.

Not all traders agree with Street in the harshness of his verdict. But there is no doubt that as Indian jewelry becomes increasingly popular, the authenticity of the turquoise used in it is being questioned more frequently.

Machine-made merchandise, plastic imitation turquoise, angers Indians who painstakingly follow procedures used by their ancestors to create turquoise jewelry. Street complains about the growing use of treated stone, derived from low-grade, chalky turquoise. It takes a knowledgeable person to tell it from real turquoise; even Indians and traders have been fooled.

This country's dwindling supply of turquoise is found in New Mexico, Arizona, Colorado, and Nevada. It forms an important part of the Indian economy in the Southwest, where master craftsmen use it in items of jewelry such as squash-blossom necklaces, beads, "bolo" ties, bracelets and rings, and belt buckles.

Machine-made, plastic jewelry cannot legally be sold in New Mexico as Indian jewelry. So it is sometimes described as "Indian-style" or "Indian-design." However,

Al R. Packard, lifelong Santa Fe trader, says he has seen Indians buy plastic jewelry from a store and then go back across the street and place the imitation items among the goods in their sidewalk vending areas.

State law says that imitation Indian arts and crafts shall be clearly designated as "Indian imitation" but the New Mexico Commission on Indian Affairs took some years to adopt a resolution that the law must be enforced.

Benny Atencio, former chairman of the All-Indian Pueblo Council at Albuquerque, says his organization is troubled "because the consumer may spend money on a product he thinks is genuine, but which is plastic."

Indians often are "wrongfully blamed" for such gyps. He says laws on the statute books could be beneficial to Indians faced with competition of machine-made products represented as genuine, Atencio explains, but there is no money to enforce the laws. He said the council will lobby for funds for enforcing existing legislation.

Rex Arrowsmith, a Santa Fe geologist and trader, says all turquoise mines produce stone of varying degrees of quality. Some is so chalky one can write with it on a blackboard. When it is treated for use in jewelry, heat and pressure impregnate colored plastic into it, simulating even the webbed lines or matrix that is highly prized.

After being treated, soft turquoise hardens to about point 4 on the hardness scale (a diamond is 10). Pure turquoise, which requires only polishing by grinding and buffing, usually has a hardness quotient of 6 or 7, sometimes 8.

Treated turquoise, in its raw form, is a lot cheaper than pure turquoise. The soft variety runs from $6 to $15 or $20 a pound; pure turquoise costs $250 a pound or more. There is no law against using or selling treated turquoise. Problems arise when people pay the price of the pure stone and get the treated one.

Spotting Turquoise Substitutes

The consensus among Indians and traders alike is that good turquoise is an excellent investment, something to be enjoyed now while it gains in value. Their advice: Know the fellow you're buying it from; be sure he's reputable.

Dealing With 'Psychic' Surgery

There are men in the Philippines who have (or claim to have) the powers to heal and/or operate on persons without instruments off any kind. They do this with no sanitation, no pain, entering the body with their hands, operating in a matter of minutes, and with prayer closing the body, leaving no scar.

—From a Travel King, Inc., promotional brochure.

WHO would believe that any man, no matter how spiritually motivated, could put his hands into your stomach or lungs and extract or neutralize diseased tissue—and all without causing pain, incision, or evidence of entry?

Some do believe. In 1973 more than 1,000 persons from the Seattle area alone paid about $1,000 apiece for a two-week "psychic pilgrimage" to the Philippines. Scores more either have gone or are planning to go. The reason: Friends have told them of miraculous cures and of new leases on life.

Some may come home apparently cured and with new hope for life, but the Federal Trade Commission (FTC) contends that's not because of any "actual surgical operation" performed by such "psychic surgeons." And on that basis the FTC obtained a Federal-court ruling halting three travel agencies' promotion of tours for afflicted persons to visit psychic surgeons in the Philippines.

The FTC action casts new light on a faith-healing practice that is being praised and damned with rising intensity.

105

Dealing With 'Psychic' Surgery

Testimonials of persons who say they have been cured are easily obtained. Many employes of the travel agencies promoting such trips say they have had afflictions treated with what their physicians here call impossible results. Nyla Ford, manager of the Travel King agency of Seattle, says she had a bone spur high on her back that had kept her from engaging in heavy exercise for years. "The day after my treatment I was swimming in the pool for the first time since an automobile accident," she says.

A dentist with cancer of the prostate says his doctors had told him he had about a year to live. "I've been over there five times now," he says, "and each time the treatment has been invaluable. My pathologist here says he can't believe that I'm still around 6½ years later."

A chiropractor says his severe astigmatism was cured, improving his eyesight to near-perfect from near-blindness.

Psychic surgery's critics are equally vocal. Dr. Ronald L. Chard, a pediatric oncologist at Children's Orthopedic Hospital in Seattle, says in an affidavit that he has been involved in the treatment of "several" children with leukemia who visited psychic surgeons: "In each of these cases I had the opportunity to observe the condition of the patients, both before and after their treatment by the 'psychic surgeons.' X-ray comparisons and other data indicated that in each case nothing was removed from the child's body. Physical examination and tests showed that no surgical operation had been performed on any of the children. In each case, with the exception of one, the chances of the child having a longer life span would have been greater if conventional medical treatment had not been significantly interrupted."

Four other physicians presented similarly damning affidavits before the court when the FTC obtained its temporary restraining order. Dan Hill, of the American Medical Association's office of investigation, says that the psychic treatment in the Philippines is "an unproven method with no medically substantiated value. Unfortunately, people deprive themselves of competent medical treatment, which [deprivation] can cause or hasten death, when they devote weeks or months to what can be an overabundance of misplaced faith. The AMA believes that faith plays a great role in healing, but a person must guard against blind faith."

Though the larger question is whether the Filipino healers actually heal, the FTC's action turns only upon whether "psychic surgery" occurs. "We aren't attempting to stop poeple from going to the Philippines," says William Erxleben, the FTC's regional director in Seattle, "but we are trying to ensure that they are getting what they bargained for. When we first got the temporary restraining order, nearly everyone who signed up for the tour leaving the next day went anyway."

Is psychic surgery possible? Contends Dr. Chard: "I would like to emphasize . . . that it is medically impossible to enter the human body and remove any tissue and close the body leaving no scar."

Still, some members of the Academy of Parapsychology and Medicine say they believe strongly in the Filipinos' treatment. Late in 1973 about 15 noted scientists, including Nobel Prize winner James D. Watson, gathered in Germany under the academy's banner to discuss psychic surgery. Says Leonard Worthington, a San Francisco lawyer on the academy's board of directors: "We have no answers, but we want to pursue follow-up studies of persons who have received the treatment. We want to be able to answer the question, finally, whether psychic healing, in general, and psychic surgery, in particular, is indeed valid treatment."

Richard Miller, director of Mankind Research Unlimited's Northwest regional office here, says that a study by the University of Washington's Department of Pathology showed that one man, Warder Bacon, probably had his body entered by the psychic surgeons. "An X-ray before he left for the Philippines shows that he had a great amount of cancerous tissue in his liver," says Miller. "When he died the liver showed no traces of cancerous tissues."

He says that not enough is known about the healers to make a positive or negative statement. "It certainly warrants a definitive study," says Miller, who also is director of the Department of Parapsychology and Paraphysics at the Experimental College at the University of Washington.

The arguments go on. A pathological study of tissue allegedly removed from a patient and brought back to this country shows it to be animal, not human, tissue. A study conducted in Washington, D.C., supposedly showed the same tissue sample was human, according to Miller.

Faith healing or psychic healing is hardly new. Sickness, pain, and approaching death can turn normally cautious, conservative people into desperate seekers of any chance to prolong life. It is a field rife with frauds and charlatans, but from Jesus Christ down through the ages to Oral Roberts and Kathryn Kuhlman of today, faith healers have attracted huge followings.

So do the Filipino psychic surgeons. It is difficult to ascertain how long the two competing religious cults in the Philippines have been practicing their treatment, but the academy's Worthington says they have been known of in this country at least since the turn of the century.

The Associated Press reported that the brother of Philippines President Ferdinand Marcos said that the psychic healers have been called to the presidential palace to treat afflicted persons at least six times in recent months. And in the past few years there have been flurries of interest in widely separated American and Canadian cities: Detroit, Chicago, Boston, San Francisco, Vancouver, and Seattle.

After reading different accounts, and seeing motion pictures of psychic surgery, I concluded the healers operate this way: They appear to be unlearned but humble, devout men. They make few pretenses, asking only for donations after completing their treatments. The donations normally range between $100 and $1,000. They supposedly are capable of discerning a person's "aura" and "energy field," mystically coming up with a diagnosis through an insight hardly similar to that employed by modern medical practitioners.

The Filipinos then begin kneading the afflicted area, working only with water and cotton. (Critics say the healers are also sleight-of-hand experts.) Then, at a crucial moment, blood spurts forth. The films are not good enough for determining fully the origin of the blood. Sometimes the surgeon produce blobs of "diseased" tissue, which some people have brought home for analysis. (Critics say the blood is concealed in dried clots between the healer's fingers, flowing only with the application of water; the tissue is said to be produced from a hiding place within the rolls of cotton.)

Treatment varies depending upon a person's ailment. Phyllis Douglass, who is 40 and has an inoperable, malignant tumor on her neck, received treatment about 10 times during her two-week tour. Her husband, Richard, accompanied her to each treatment session. His affidavit forms much of the cause of action for the FTC.

Douglass is a painting contractor who has seen his business and his financial reserves dwindle away because of his wife's illness. "we decided to go because two of our best friends had been there," he says, sipping coffee in their comfortable home overlooking Puget Sound. "They swore that his life had been saved by Rev. Tony [leader of one of two cults of healers]. We wanted to believe, we wanted Phyllis to be healed, we really did."

Douglass says that he went fully prepared to document the amazing recovery of his wife. "I wrote down what I had witnessed each day, how she felt, and what Rev. Tony said. I also took some movies of him in action. It disturbed him, but it didn't stop him from working on her that day.

"I also had brought along a bottle of formaldehyde because I wanted to able to preserve whatever tissue he might extract from her. When he did pull this bunch of stuff out of her, I just grabbed it from his hand and stuck it in a bottle. I wanted to prove to myself that my wife had been cured."

Douglass says now that he had begun to be disillusioned while they were still in the Philippines. In Hawaii, however, Mrs. Douglass sent the specimen to her doctor, E.G. Burgwald, commenting: "Feeling so good we decided to stop in Maui for 10 days. At present time am not taking any pain pills." At home, she miles ruefully and says: "That was the only time in months. Actually I was feeling good until the day I saw Dr. Burgwald after I returned home. I could tell from his face that the tissue wasn't what it was supposed to be." It wasn't. It was animal tissue, according to a patholgy report.

Psychic surgery is an emotional issue. There have

been no authoritative studies of it. AMA statistics show, says Miller, that persons who have terminal cancer have a one-in-five recovery rate, even after the bad news is pronounced. "The key will be to determine what percentage of persons who have been treated in the Philippines recover," says Miller, who adds that he is working to have a follow-up study started.

The FTC action has little to do with the question of whether psychic surgery works. As many fans of Rev. Tony and his colleagues say, it doesn't matter if surgery occurs; what matters is whether healing occurs, and that isn't at issue. The FTC hearing will determine whether surgery is performed and whether three travel agencies deceived customers with promotional efforts. The FTC's Erxleben says it is likely that if the commission's complaint is upheld, persons who took the tour could receive refunds from the travel agencies.

"It is a difficult situation," remarks the dentist, who says he doesn't want his name published because of his profession's attitude toward psychic healers. "Even the healers wouldn't tell you that they are successful all of the time. I understand that if they get too commercial or misuse their powers, they lose their abilities. I've heard, when I was over there, that some of them can open the body, but then they either can't bring the diseased tissue to the surface for extraction or can't close the body up again.

"I have faith in the psychic surgeons, but not enough faith that I have discontinued my cobalt or female-hormone treatments. You know, the tours are valuable because if a person were to go over by himself, he might not be able to find the healers, and he would need, because he would prbably be quite sick, the convenience and savings of a group tour."

111

Dealing With 'Psychic' Surgery

Despite rising interest in psychic phenomena and arguments about whether psychic surgeons actually operate or can even cure anyone, the controversy here underscores a problem that may never be resolved by any court: The emergence of healers such as psychic surgeons presents seriously ill—and sometimes desperate— people with the question of whether to spend large amounts of savings and perhaps interrupt regular medical treatment in order to seek such help. Their quest may even worsen their illness.

"That is the great trouble," says the AMA's Hill. "we have numerous cases on record where people felt they had been cured and then died shortly afterward from the disease of which they said they had been cured. We know faith has a great role in healing. We do not know how great a role faith healers have, if any."

Wrong Numbers on Yellow Pages

Let your fingers do the walking," runs the familiar Bell System slogan urging customers to do their shopping through the Yellow Pages of telephone books, where businesses and services are listed by category.

A less familiar message voiced by critics of the Yellow Pages is that you may get those fingers burned by unscrupulous businessmen who advertise in your local telephone directory.

"If you let your fingers do the walking through the Yellow Pages, you may find that some very unsavory characters have walked into your life," Bess Myerson, former New York City consumer-affairs commissioner, has said.

The Yellow Pages have been touted as reliable where-to-buy-it guides since World War II. But critics contend that local telephone companies affiliated with the Bell System do not exercise sufficient control over the advertisements they accept and print.

Top telephone-company officials disagree. "With 18 million ads a year in Bell System directories, we can't check them all as closely as we'd like," says a supervisor of Yellow Pages Sales for the American Telephone and Telegraph Co. (AT&T). "But we don't have any bigger problem with trust than any other part of the media. By and large, most of our advertising copy is fairly straightforward."

There are certain "problem areas," AT&T acknowledges. Primarily they are in categories where companies offer consumer services, such as appliance repairs and household moving.

Representatives of local consumer-affairs departments and Better Business Bureaus say that there are many other "problem areas" where misleading advertising is common, such as home improvements, vocational education, and auto driving courses. And the kinds of misleading advertising permitted, they say, are exceeded only by the ingenuity of the advertisers themselves. Examples of misleading Yellow Pages practices cited by these critics include:

● Unlicensed companies or persons are sometimes permitted to list themselves as members of licensed professions. A New York Telephone Co. official estimates that 8 or 9 per cent of the company's listings under "physicians and surgeons" are not licensed by the state of New York. A California Department of Consumer Affairs spokesman said that unlicensed odd-job handymen listed under the same heading as licensed contractors are one of his office's biggest sources of complaints.

● One company may run several display ads using different names. The QQQ Washing Machine Repair Co., for a fictitious example, might run one ad using that name and place other ads using the names "QQQ Service Center" and "Quality Appliance Repairs." Together, the ads might occupy a large share of the available display space under "washing machines," thereby increasing the likelihood that the consumer will respond to at least one of the ads. Even worse, the unsuspecting reader of the Yellow Pages might speak to the same company three times, getting the same estimate each time.

● A frequent accompaniment to multiple listing is

for the advertiser to declare in each of his ads that he provides service on only one brand, promising, for example, "service only on Kenmore" in one ad, and "service only on Whirlpool" in another. The customer gets the impression that he is dealing with a specialty company, one that is more likely to be able to handle his problem than a company servicing many brands. In a variation of this technique, the advertiser may falsely claim that he is an "authorized representative" of a major manufacturer.

● Address information, or the lack of it, is a source of problems, particularly in large cities where directories serving various sections of the city are printed. An advertiser may place an ad in each of the smaller directories, indicating that he provides service for that area while, in fact, he has only one downtown location. If no address is provided, the customer may think he is dealing with a neighborhood establishment.

In one New York case, a television-repair company advertised four ficitious local addresses in the Yellow Pages. The company sent "repairmen" to the homes of customers and hauled off their television sets to perform what invariably turned out to be exorbitantly expensive repairs. The unfortunate consumer had no idea where his set really was, and , until paying, could not even get near his set to see whether the repairs were needed or preformed.

Few critics suggest that telephone companies knowingly permit fictitious or erroneous information to appear in the Yellow Pages. The main problem, critics say, is that telephone companies fail to check advertising copy thoroughly enough, and once the Yellow Pages are printed, any mistake stays around for at least a year.

A telephone company spokesman replies that it does check copy, but not necessarily all the items its critics would like.

"We don't go out and investigate each advertiser," says an AT&T official, "but every advertisement we accept must meet a high set of standards set forth by the Better Business Bureau. We concentrate on determining whether what the advertiser says in his ad is accurate, rather than trying to determine whether his operation is fraudulent."

Among the items AT&T says are checked: the advertiser's use of superlatives ("We won't let anyone say he's the 'biggest' or the 'oldest' unless he can prove it"); the promise of a guarantee ("All conditions must be spelled out, or the word 'conditional' used"); and publication of prices ("We don't permit it: Prices fluctuate too much over the length of time a directory is in use").

A serious criticism leveled against the Yellow Pages is that even when repeated complaints or actual charges of fraud are brought against a company, the telephone company may continue to permit it to buy ads.

To that, a spokesman replies: "When a firm is convicted of fraudulent trade practices, we certainly abide by that, and remove him from the directory, but we face a problem if there's no ruling. Who are we to judge whether, when a customer complains, it's a real case of fraud or just a mistake? We try to be fair with both the consumer and the advertiser, but we are not a police department or an investigative agency."

The solution, says AT&T, is for the government to put fraudulent operations out of business and for professional associations to alert the telephone company if an unlicensed advertiser turns up in the Yellow Pages.

Not all parts of the Bell System think this is enough, though. The New York Telephone Co., beginning in 1973, put into effect a wide range of new standards aimed at reducing the problem of misleading advertising. The standards were developed in consultation with the New York City Department of Consumer Affairs, where an official calls the changes "very important."

Under the new standards, companies are not allowed to state that they have branches in several parts of the city unless this is true. All advertisements have to feature an address where a responsible member of the business can be reached. Advertisers under "problem headings," such as "moving and storage," are checked to verify that they hold valid licenses. Multiple listings under different names are permitted only if the ads state that all the names refer to the same business, and claims of exclusive servicing on more than one brand will be prohibited. Claims of authorization are checked with the manufacturer. And special problems are being handled through a consumer-protection telephone service, a directory advertising review Board, and a Yellow Pages editor.

"Obviously this is going to be an expensive and time consuming undertaking," says a New York Telephone directory manager. "But we have some problems in New York that we don't have in other parts of the country, and if this is what it takes to maintain the quality of our product, then I think this is what we have to do.

Consumer advocates and local Better Business Bureaus offer several tips on ways consumers can make the Yellow Pages more useful:

✔ If a company or individual is listed under a category licensed by your state or local government, ask for the license number or check credentials with the licensing agency.

✔ If it's an individual or a small business your're considering, ask for references. No matter what the size of the business, it's always a good idea to go where poeple you know have come away satisfied. If you'll be signing a contract, consult with a lawyer if the amount involved seems significant to you.

✔ Your local Better Business Bureau, Chamber of Commerce, or consumer agency may be able to provide helpful information. Check how long the company has been in business, what sort of complaints have been lodged against it, how it's handled those complaints.

✔ Don't rely only on the size of an ad. Bigness does not necessarily mean trustworthiness.

✔ Perhaps most important, don't forget that timeless piece of advice, "Let the buyer beware."

As a phone-company man puts it: "The consumer has to face the fact that there *are* a few unscrupulous business people. There always have been, and there always will be. We're trying to keep them out of the Yellow Pages, but the user must always maintain his sense of caution."

The Dance School Whirl

USUALLY I'm considered a pretty good dancer. I'm not fancy, but I can keep time to the music, improvise simple steps, and look as though I'm enjoying myself—which I generally am.

For four weeks, though, I couldn't tell my left foot from my right. I stumbled over my partner's feet. I strode forward when I should have glided backward. A rhapsody of grace I wasn't.

I was a student at a franchised dance studio. I enrolled because I wanted to learn why items like this kept popping up in the newspapers:

Austin, Texas—A 56 year-old widow, sold her home and used the proceeds of her husband's life-insurance policy to buy $27,000 worth of dancing lessons and $10,000 worth of stock at a Fred Astaire dance studio.

Why did some dance studios command such trust and such sums? I wondered. The painful memories of former clients held a few clues:

"I was lonely," the Austin widow testified in a suit to recover her money. "My husband had passed away. I had no social life, and when I went to this studio they were very friendly and loving, and in an intimate atmosphere they would tell me: 'You want to be a great dancer? You are going to be the best.'

"And they would flatter me and play upon my emotional status as a lonely widow to induce me to buy more lessons, and I kept getting in deeper . . . ."

119

The Dancing School Whirl

Well, I'm not elderly and I'm not lonely, but I thought I could feign loneliness to see firsthand how the dance-studio game is played. I chose Arthur Murray, Inc., because by coincidence its local studios were running a "special"—$88 worth of lessons for only $10. So, wearing out-of-style clothes, acting shy and timid, and posing as an unemployed, new-in-town secretary, I enrolled in the Arlington, Va., Arthur Murray studio.

Following is an abbreviated version of the diary I kept:

FIRST NIGHT—Miss Lee, the slim smooth-spoken supervisor, greets me warmly and introduces me to my teacher, Mr. Markland. Tall. Bearded. Friendly. Wears bright-colored jackets. Holds my hand a lot. He explains he's going to evaluate my dancing ability.

After my first feeble attempts to pick up the fox trot and cha-cha, we return to Miss Lee's office. She checks my completed "dance-evaluation form," tells me I have good rhythm and balance but need to improve my self-confidence and my ability to follow.

"Dancing will do a lot for you," she tells me. "It will put more fun in your life, give you poise, make you more comfortable at parties, make you a better date." She suggests I apply my current $88 program toward a program of 20 private and 20 group lessons. Normally $700, the program would cost me only $612.

"I think I'd like to think about it," I stammer.

SECOND NIGHT—Mr. Markland greets me with a big smile. He shows me the Magic Step and Magic Turn. "What makes it magic?" I ask.

"I don't know," he laughs. "We had to call it something."

I suddenly notice I'm trying to learn the cha-cha to waltz music—"Edelweiss," I think— and other people are dancing the rhumba and the swing. "Oh, you have to ignore the music," Mr. Markland explains. "If you learn to dance to the music, you concentrate too much on whether you're hitting the right beat and you don't learn your dancing right. You have to work up to dancing with the music."

Mr. Markland jokes and flirts with me. When I hold myself too far away, he tells me to "get close enough for me to bite your ear." Later he hands me a form and asks me to check the major reasons I want to learn to dance. My top choices: "have more fun out of life," "increase popularity," and "make more friends."

THIRD NIGHT—My first "social-practice session," the Arthur Murray equivalent of a party. The mirror-paneled ballroom is transformed into an intimate night club, complete with small tables, net-covered candles, and refreshments—a nonalcoholic fruit punch.

Most of the 40 or so students are middle-aged or older. A retired teacher tells me the lessons are well worth the money—even the $2,000 she has spent in the last year—because, "If people didn't do this, they'd just sit in their rooms."

After about an hour, awards are given out. The winner of the "Tournament of Champions" is presented a trophy. He won by buying the most lessons and bringing in the most new guests who also purchased lessons, Mr. Markland explains.

FOURTH NIGHT—Mr. Markland teaches me the Arthur Murray and Kathryn Murray Turns. Between steps we talk. He asks if I have a boy friend. I say no, why does he ask.

"Because it's part of my profession to ask questions. They may seem personal, but they're important to my designing the right program to fill your needs. If you're lonely, we want to teach you to dance well enough so you'll be more confident and will meet people."

We sit down, and he brings out a large notebook. "How well do you want to be able to dance?" he asks. "Just enough to be comfortable at parties, or enough to perform?" He seems to be reading from an instruction sheet.

"I think I'd just like to be able to dance at parties."

"Ah, that's the 'Comfortable-Confident' level! That will take from 25 to 35 hours of instruction for each of our four basic dances, for a total of 100 to 140 hours."

FIFTH NIGHT—Mr. Markland teaches me the rhumba and the swing. Halfway through the hour, Miss Lee wants to know if I'm interested in becoming a "Comfortable-Confident" dancer.

"That depends on how much it costs," I reply.

"You can't look at this just in terms of cost," she smiles. "We're talking in the neighborhood of what it might cost to buy a car—say, $3,000—but consider how much more dancing lessons will do for your life than a car! A car depreciates after a few years, it starts needing repairs, and then what do you have? But with dancing, its value *ap*preciates. Why not spend the same money for something that will really change your life?"

I say that sounds like a lot of money for an unemployed secretary, and I rejoin Mr. Markland on the dance floor.

"I know dancing lessons could do a lot for you," he says. "You're at the age where your friends will all be getting married, and you'll be going to lots of weddings and formals, and you'll want to meet the 'upper people,' not just the kind you meet in bars."

"Do that many young men dance the type of dances taught at Arthur Murray?"

"Well, frankly, no—but you won't always be young,

and when you really get into a meaningful relationship with a man, he'll want you to be able to dance."

SIXTH NIGHT—The end of the line: Tonight I get my "progress report."

"Hey, you look sharp," Mr. Markland says. My baggy skirt and blouse clash.

We practice our dances, all to Latin music. He shows me the program he has designed for me—a total of 119 hours. He and Miss Lee then take me to a small, cold room off the main ballroom.

"Do you want to continue dancing?" she asks me.

"Yes, if it's not too expensive."

"Do you have confidence in Arthur Murray's methods of instruction?"

"I guess so."

"Do you have confidence in yourself to learn to dance?"

"I'm not sure."

"If you had to rate your desire to complete the dance program on a scale of 1 to 10, with 10 the highest, how would you rate it?"

"Oh, I guess about 8."

"Okay, let's see what you've learned." Miss Lee puts on some records, and Mr. Markland and I show her how well I've learned the waltz, the fox trot, the rhumba, and the cha-cha. The only problem: Since this is the first time I've done each dance to the proper music, I can't keep time.

Next we go into Miss Lee's office. The recommended course of 119 hours costs about $3,300, she says, but I can take it in "chunks." With the $88 discount from the mini-course I've already taken, plus a $23 discount I somehow merit, this $700 chunk will cost me only $589. And if I can't pay it all now, I can pay $89 down and the rest over 12 months at 1½ per cent interest a month.

When I hesitate, she cuts the down payment to $49 and finally to zero if I'll just sign the contract she hastily writes up. She doesn't tell me, nor does she write in the contract, the yearly interest rate or other information required by the Truth-in-Lending Act.

I hem and haw. "That sounds like an awful lot of money. Maybe I should wait until I have a job."

"It's quite a saving if you take it now," Mr. Markland says reassuringly.

"Can't I think it over?" I plead. I'm beginning to feel tense.

No, they say, because my sessions have ended, I have to decide tonight: It's an Arthur Murray rule.

After about half an hour Mr. Markland takes me into another room, where we continue to discuss the great deal I'm getting. I ask to take the unsigned contract home with me. He says I can't.

"It sounds like you don't really want to learn to dance," he reproaches me.

"No, it's not that," I say "but I didn't expect I'd have to decide tonight."

We exchange mournful good-bys, and I run all the way home. An hour later Mr. Markland calls me. He has talked to Miss Lee; she'll make an exception for me. I can still get the discount if I sign up within the next two days. I thank him gratefully and hang up.

Later I called George Theiss, president of Arthur Murray, Inc. Theiss, who oversees the company's 225 franchised studios from Coral Gables, Fla., was perturbed to hear of my experience but insisted it was an "isolated example." Arthur Murray's, he said, is "trying to get away from the gigolo approach and the lonely-hearts atmosphere." Noting that the company has had problems with the studios in this locale for years, Theiss promised to send a "franchise representative " to the studio immediately to check it out.

Remember, it wasn't because I suspected anything that I enrolled at Arthur Murray's. Indeed, the Federal Trade Commission (FTC) and Better Business Bureau report no current complaints against the Arlington school. The treatment I got was actually mild compared with the tactics of some studios that have gotten in trouble with the law. Some of those tactics, as described in various law suits and FTC decisions, include:

● Selling students phone stock in the dance studio and then persuading them to turn it in for more lessons.

● Bugging students' conversations, using hidden listening devices.

● Selling overlapping contracts, so that no sooner does the student sign one contract than he or she is pressured to sign a new, costlier one. The student never is sure how much is owed.

● Selling "lifetime" contracts to elderly people for so many hours of instruction that the signers could not reasonably expect to live that long.

Unscrupulous studios do not have to resort to means such as these, though. There is no substitute for the simple hard-soft sell: excessive flattery and attentions from young, attractive teachers, combined with emotional, high-pressured sales pitches that play upon students' needs and insecurities.

Generally, those who fall for such tactics are the elderly, say consumer-protection officials. Often they've just lost a loved one and are looking for companionship. And more often than not they're widows who've been left a "nest egg" to live out their lives.

"What you get then is a lot of lonely old people buying a social relationship," says one FTC lawyer. "There's a very strong element of sex in this, but it's surrogate sex; there's nothing overt. All these people want is to be flattered, to feel wanted by someone of the opposite sex."

The FTC has been one of the severest critics of dance studios' high-pressure practices. Since 1960 it has ordered Arthur Murray studios twice and Fred Astaire studios once to "cease and desist" from such techniques. A smattering of states in recent years—among them California, Illinois, and New York—have outlawed lifetime contracts and other flagrant abuses.

It is difficult to determine, however, whether abuses have declined. Neither the FTC nor the Council of Better Business Bureaus maintains a complaint file on such matters. Checks with attorneys general and consumer-protection bureaus in California, New York, Wisconsin, Illinois, Oregon, Kentucky, and Pennsylvania reveal recent or current complaints in most of those states, but most complaints pertain to only one or two studios.

"It doesn't appear to be an industry-wide problem," says James D. Jeffries, assistant attorney general of Wisconsin. An FTC spokesman, however, calls it a "recurrent problem."

Theiss of Arthur Murray says most of the abuses within his company occurred about 20 years ago but that "new ideas of consumer relations" have since taken hold.

Now, he says, the company sends four "franchise representatives" around the country to spot-check studios, forbids studios to sell dance contracts of more than 200 hours, requires a three-day concellation clause in all contracts, and gives refunds even after three days if a student is unhappy. Since the mid-1960s, he says, the company has canceled its agreement with 35 per cent of its franchisees for failing to meet the company standards.

Chester Casanave, president of Ronby Corp., which

franchises the 100 or so Fred Astaire studios, acknowledges that "occasional bad pennies get into the business" but says: "We get them out. Maybe three or four students over the course of a year will be unhappy with their programs, but hundreds more will be happy.

"The industry does a great service for people," Casanave adds, "especially older people. As people get older, they become unwanted. A lot of them have a great deal of money, but money doesn't give them comfort or love. The dance studio gives them a social life, makes them feel they're not just a bump on a log."

Critics disagree with Casanave's view of both the size of the problem and the value of the service. They say many would-be complainants are too embarrassed to come forward. And Robert Nicholas, deputy attorney general in the Pennsylvania Bureau of Consumer Protection, suggests that the abuses pose an ethical question too. "No one objects to someone selling dancing lessons," he says. "But why sell someone 75 years old 10 years' worth of lessons?"

Keeping Veterans' Records

A fire on the sixth floor of the National Military Personnel Records Center, St. Louis, started July 12, 1973, and was not brought under control until the following day. The sixth floor contained 21.8 million sets of records covering all Army veterans discharged between Nov. 1, 1912, and Dec. 31, 1959 (that period covers the Mexican Border War, World War I, World War II, and the Korean War). Also stored on the floor were records for Air Force veterans with surnames beginning with I through Z who were discharged between Sept. 25, 1947, and Dec. 31, 1963.

If you are in either group, the probability is that your military records are damaged beyond recovery, although some records are being restored.

What of the 15 or 16 million veterans whose records can't be restored? How can they or their survivors establish eligibility for Federal benefits for veterans, such as burial allowances?

"At the time of the fire we advised everyone that the loss of the St. Louis records would have very little impact on veterans' claims," says S. M. Appleman, the Veterans Administration's director of press relations.

Appleman adds that if a veteran filed a claim prior to the fire the VA would have his medical records.

The VA also has records, despite the fire, for any veteran who ever applied for Governement (GI) life insurance, who ever went to school under the GI Bill, who ever

128

applied for a GI home or business loan, or who ever filed any kind of compensation claim.

If a veteran has absolutely no personal military records but can remember his serial number, he can be traced through records from various military stations where he served.

Veterans and their families who are faced with an emergency should remember that most states have state-operated veterans-affairs offices. An officer at each state location has direct access to the St. Louis Records Center, and he can obtain information more successfully than can an individual.

CUSTOMERS AT ABOUT 1,000 stores, banks and service firms in the United States and overseas are being asked to "personalize" as well as sign their checks.

The customer touches thumb to the back of his check. The check is then slipped into a black device about the size of a brick. A clerk touches a lever and the thumbprint in permanently outlined on the check.

The check then follows routine bank processing. If the check is valid, the thumbprint remains simply a memento of honest business. If the check is rejected by the bank as fraudulent, the instrument with its incriminating evidence is turned over to the local police department for a search through fingerprint files.

Identicator Corp. of San Francisco, which manufactures the print device, reports an encouraging demand for its product. The success of the process, according to Identicator President Oscar Pieper, is its simplicity. There is no need to impress the thumb on a chemical pad or use pre-treated paper to obtain the impression. Says Pieper:

"When we ask a customer to touch the back of a check—personalize is the term we prefer—he leaves a latent print. The device has a dry chemical process that makes it instantly visible. There is no mess."

Since its introduction in 1972, he says the system has been well received by the public. "Honest people are aware of fraud and willing to help stop ripoffs."

Look Before You Bite

 BEFORE you bite into that luscious peanut-chocolate bar, pause and look it over: Some insects find nuts alluring and may have spotted your candy bar first. It's "not uncommon" to find them or their eggs or fecal matter in candy and other processed foods, according to officials at the Food and Drug Administration.

"There is no health hazard involved though it is esthetically objectionable," says Norman Kramer, chief of the compliance branch at the FDA's district office in Baltimore. Kramer says his office each week receives one or two complaints about insect remains out of 25 to 30 consumer complaints of all types. The FDA does not, however, compile national statistics on insect complaints.

Infestation usually occurs in warehouses. The culprit is usually one of several species of moths that are attracted to nuts. The moths and some close relatives also will penetrate packages of spices, dried fruits such as raisins, and processed grain products, such as noddles or cereal. Red pepper is actually the first choice of most pests, says William V. Eisenberg, chief of the microanalytical branch of FDA's office of sciences. But nuts are a very close second and much more widely distributed in foods. Black pepper, incidentally, is far down the list.

Eisenberg explains that the moths lay their eggs on or near packages of food. When the tiny larvae hatch, they can easily penetrate the packaging. After feeding for a period, the worms leave the food to spin a cocoon and metamorphose into adult moths. Eisenberg says eggs sometimes are attached to nuts before they are processed and hatch later inside packages.

A consumer who discovers signs of infestation should keep the food and its container and report the incident to the FDA and the local health department. An FDA inspector may want to obtain a sample for analysis as well as packaging codes. After investigation locally, complaints are sent to the FDA office nearest the point of processing. Complaints about one product from several parts of the country indicate trouble at the factory rather than on warehouse or store shelves.

Making the BBB Work

OVER the years some unhappy consumers have wondered what the Better Business Bureau is better than. They rarely ask such questions in Akron, Ohio, where the Better Business Bureau has become probably the best anywhere. There the BBB is helping a tough county prosecutor put crooks in jail and get defrauded consumers their money back.

The county prosecutor's office, working with the local BBB, has won convictions of, or obtained guilty pleas in one 10-month period from: a heating and cooling contractor, a carpet installer, a paving contractor, a Honda dealer, a car dealer, an aluminum-siding installer, a home-improvement contractor, and some sellers of a piece of baby furniture called Stroll-O-Chair.

About 11:30 o'clock one night, a door-to-door salesman got Mr. and Mrs. Richard Kelly to sign their name to a $570 contract for a Stroll-O-Chair, a contraption that transforms into 14 different pieces of baby furniture. The Kellys hadn't been sure they wanted it, since the salesman didn't bring along a sample for them to inspect.

But he reassured them, says Rita Kelly, that "since we were a nice couple and he was a nice guy, he was going to have the furniture delivered to his house and was going to write 'Satisfaction Guaranteed' on the contract. That way he'd bring the furniture from his house to our house. If we didn't like it, we wouldn't be out anything, because we could cancel the contract."

That seemed like a fair deal. Besides, Mrs. Kelly was expecting a baby soon, the Stroll-O-Chair would save room in their cramped mobile home in Cuyahoga Falls, Ohio, a suburb of Akron, and Kelly, a radio-TV repairman, had just received a raise. So they bought it.

Next day when the Kellys decided they could live without a $570 Stroll-O-Chair and called the salesman to cancel the order, Rita Kelly recalls "he got nasty." Just how could they back out when they hadn't seen the product? he wanted to know. So they went over to see it. It was "very clumsy," says Mrs. Kelly. "I didn't think it was as safe as he made it out to be, and that was one of his big selling points."

After some haggling, the salesman said the Kellys were bound by the contract (the fine print said they couldn't cancel it) and that the furniture was on its way to their home. A young boy showed up with a big box a few days later and wouldn't leave until Mrs. Kelly called a cop, who ordered the boy off her property.

Mrs. Kelly called Jasper Rowland, director of Akron's Better Business Bureau, who wanted a complete report from her—to make a speech, she thought.

"I'm ashamed to say, I turned chicken," says Mrs. Kelly. The Kellys knew that their contract had been sold to a finance company, which would be harder to drive off than a delivery boy. They certainly didn't expect the BBB to stand up to the finance company for them. They never sent the BBB their report.

Months later, Mrs. Kelly says, she danced through the house when she read that a grand jury had indicted the Stroll-O-Chair salesman and four colleagues. The indictments were based on testimony by a number of other people whose complaints had been plucked by the prosecutor from the BBB's files. The news prompted Mrs. Kelly to testify and additional indictments followed. The sellers pleaded guilty to obtaining money under false pretenses, agreeing to make restitution to the Akron-area customers they had lured into their contracts.

The Akron BBB got tough in 1972, shortly after a newly elected Summit County prosecutor, Stephen Gabalac, took office. Gabalac is an energetic young lawyer who worked for 10 years as an assistant county prosecutor before his election to the top spot. He says he never realized consumers had such serious problems until he started investigating murders. Yes, murders.

He'd be out at 2:30 a.m. taking statements from witnesses to stabbings, shootings, beatings; and in the midst of all the blood and confusion witnesses often would say something like: "Look, you're a lawyer from the prosecutor's office. I took my car into so-and-so's garage and they told me the repair job would cost $20; but when I picked it up they hit me with a $60 bill."

"Here these people had just witnessed a major crime," says Gabalac, "and these consumer problems are what concerned them." Gabalac heard stories from people who thought TV-repair shops had cheated them, or who thought several thousand dollars was too much to pay someone for doing a little work on their leaky basement.

Some months after he was elected, Gabalac got together with the BBB's Rowland and told Rowland he wanted to go after shady businesses that were conning Akron consumers. Could the Better Business Bureau help? For Jasper Rowland the cavalry had arrived at last.

Rowland has been a BBB man since 1950 and at times it has been frustrating work. As the agent of business' official self-regulatory mechanism, Rowland says he is usually successful in ironing out problems between businessmen and consumers. But the really bad operators usually told him to just shove off.

"In the past," Rowland says, "whenever we'd get something that looked awfully bad, we went to a prosecutor, and he'd say, 'What law is being violated?'" The BBB didn't know, says Rowland, who, like most BBB officers, isn't a lawyer. "We just knew that people were being harmed." He says the prosecutors were usually too busy: "They've got murders, robberies, and rapes to handle."

Another thing most prosecutors have is a limited budget. When Summit County told Gabalac it couldn't give him any money to set up a consumer division, he talked to the head of a student-intern program at the University of Akron Law School. Two law students, whose pay would be three credit hours at the end of the quarter, were assigned to the prosecutor. Gabalac, assistant prosecutor Stanley Aronson, and the two student investigators dropped by Rowland's office to see what he had for them.

He had a file on Stroll-O-Chair salesmen a foot high. He had computerized files on a lot of people, collected solely from complaining consumers. From a metropolitan area of about 500,000 people, the local BBB gets about 80,000 calls yearly. One file had to do with a paving contractor, and Gabalac's "Fraud Squad," as they named themselves, picked him for their first time at bat.

The contractor primarily worked the homes of the elderly, telling them he would pave their driveways with asphalt or cement, settling for whatever price he could talk them into; generally it was between $400 and $600. He would return about the first of the month, when Social Security checks arrive, take a "down payment" of $100, throw some dirt around, and disappear.

Investigators persuaded a number of the contractor's victims, who had complained to the BBB, to tell their story to a grand jury, which indicted the contractor for larceny by trick, a felony in Ohio. He went to prison.

Other "victims" of Gabalac's Fraud Squad include: a heating and colling contractor who was throwing smoke bombs into good furnaces to simulate defective operation, then ripping the furnaces apart for "repairs" before the horrified home owner could think to have the local utility inspect the furnace; a large Honda dealer who was selling three-year-old motorcycles and demonstrators as new (he paid restitution for them); an auto dealer who was setting odometers back on used rental cars and demonstrators (local auto dealers told Gabalac that "everyone does it," but he told them that from now on no one would do it); and a home-improvement company, in business in the area since 1952, which advertised "specials" as a come-on, then put up cheap mahogany-veneer wallboard and cheap ceiling material, charging $5,000 for the job.

Gabalac has made cheating consumers a major crime in Akron, mostly because he generally charges people in the consumer area with felonies such as larceny by trick or obtaining money under false pretenses. Rowland attributes much of Gabalac's success to his reliance on harder-to-prove felony charges, which carry the possibility of a long prison sentence, rather than misdemeanors.

"The threat of jail for a bad operator is much worse than the threat of a slap on the wrist that most of them get under the state and Federal laws governing specific business practices," says Rowland.

About every two weeks Rowland has lunch with Anthony Cardarelli, whom Gabalac talked away from his job at the Goodyear Tire & Rubber Co. earlier this year to manage his growing consumer division (the law school keeps it supplied with free investigators). "One of my problems," says Rowland, "is to feed things in sort of a regulated way. We have a backlog here, and we don't want to swamp them."

Rowland contends that Gabalac's success has given the Akron BBB a respect it never got previously from the local business community. Now businessmen call him regularly to find out if his files depict them as good guys or bad guys, or to ask his opinion of something they're going to do.

Both Rowland and Gabalac take pains to avoid sounding like antibusiness head-hunters. "We know that 99 per cent of all business is good," Rowland says, "but that 1 per cent is truly bad." Gabalac concurs, adding that they're helping not only consumers but also legitimate business men who have to compete with the crooks.

What these two have done by uniting really, is to give Akron's consumers a much cleaner market place than either office could achieve on its own. Despite the heavy legal club carried by most prosecutors, their chances of winning a case against a fraudulent businessman are less than one might imagine. Obtaining an indictment from a grand jury generally requires solid proof that someone has been cheating many people over a period of time. Collecting that much evidence is a costly, time-consuming job that many prosecutors' offices can't afford. Enter the Better Business Bureau and its huge files filled with just the evidence a prosecutor needs.

Job-Hunting Problem:
Overqualification

THOUSANDS of new college graduates, degrees in hand, invade employment offices, confidently awaiting a choice of jobs. Many are shocked to hear, "You're overqualified.

Meanwhile, up the employment scale, middle-aged people with years of experience, yet also yearning for a new challenge and a more satisfying life, hear the same refrain: "We can't touch you; you're overqualified."

Overqualification: Is it a phenomenon of a too-specialized society, or an all-purpose alibi for any-purpose rejection? Is it a myth nurtured by overly skeptical employers, or a justifiable barrier to the job seeker?

It was certainly no myth to a 34-year-old Pennsylvanian. He had a bachelor's degree from the University of Illinois and a master's from Wisconsin. He taught at a Pennsylvania college for almost two years but the pay was poor and frustration set in.

Seeking more money, he applied for a production-line job at Hofmann Industries in Sinking Spring, Pa. He had heard that the company disliked hiring college graduates for blue-collar jobs. So he omitted his college background and teaching experience from his application.

He got the job, but then was identified as an activist in a company strike several months later. An investigation uncovered his credentials gap, and he was fired. He was rehired after a labor arbitrator ruled he had been wronged.

"Any college-trained man might understandably be vexed to know that he would be denied employment because he was 'over-educated' for a blue-collar job," the arbitrator commented. "The company's position that a man who has been educated in college is not likely to make a reliable blue-collar employe was not substantiated by any credible evidence."

Evidence *is* slim, for there have been few studies, or even thoughtful dialog, on overqualification. But most employers and employment agencies consider it bad personnel policy to hire people whose education or experience is more than the job requires.

"I interviewed a young lady today for a clerical job," explains a personnel executive for a large manufacturing company. "She would sit and file all day and do some very minor typing. She's got a college degree. Chances are she's not going to be interested in the job very long. She's going to get bored, and you're going to see that in morale, you're going to see that in absenteeism, and we don't want to take those risks."

In the employer's view, these are the reasons the cards are stacked against overqualified applicants:

High turnover—Even menial jobs require a breaking-in period, which costs the company time and money. A job that doesn't use a worker's abilities probably will be used only as a stop-gap base for more job-hunting. The company's training investment will be lost.

Poor morale—There's little motivation to be productive. "I see the ways college-educated men in the factory play games with the foremen," says an employer's spokesman, "and they're out absent or they become what they call in the factory 'latrine lawyers,' spending all their time reading the company contract or becoming involved in the union negotiations—little John L. Lewises."

Employers really don't like to talk about the over-qualification problem. It smacks of discrimination, and Federal law prohibits denying an applicant a job because of race, color, creed, sex, or age. Companies found guilty of such violations have been fined hundreds of thousands of dollars.

But there is evidence that overqualification may sometimes be used as an excuse for rejection on other grounds. A company doesn't want a female office manager? Tell any woman she's overqualified. Qualms about a black on the staff? Tell the black applicant he's too good for the job. An applicant is older than you would like? His experience clearly overqualifies him.

Some employers proscribe overqualification as a job barrier. The Chesapeake & Potomac Telephone Co. (C&P), one of the Washington, D.C., area's largest employers, specifically forbids it, although its instructions to job interviewers add that "applicants holding degrees should be informed of management programs and referred to management employment if they are interested and if openings exist."

C&P's service-representative position is a middle-range nonmanagement job for which demand is steady. These workers take service orders, handle complaints, and answer questions about billing. Traditionally they've been non-college people.

"There is an increasing trend for the 'overqualified' coming into this position," says J. S. Gillespie, a C&P executive. "Last year 31 per cent of the hires were college graduates."

But the trend is not without problems, substantiating employers' fears. During four months in 1973, half of the service representatives who quit were college graduates, and two-thirds of the other resignees had some college work.

"A college degree is not required for any job we have," the C&P official notes. "But I have to say that [this policy] has added to our problems as far as turnover is concerned."

Overqualification affects young people most noticeably each spring, when the graduating crop doffs cap and gown to enter the job market. Dr. Albert F. Furbay of Western Michigan State University's School of Communications has seen the action from both the campus and from employment agencies.

"A lot of kids say: 'Well, it doesn't look like I'll get a job teaching. What else can I do?'" says Furbay. "They go in for interviews, and it's almost like they have a neon sign right on their forehead that says: 'This is only temporary. As soon as I get a teaching job I'm going to leave you.'

"Personnel people disqualify applicants, rather than qualify them, in order to narrow the field. If with my degree I communicate to them I really wouldn't be happy in this job, then they have a perfect right to say, 'I don't think you'll be happy in this job.'"

"The real talents of a college graduate get lost in the discussion. What does a college graduate have? Well, he has the ability to learn, to grow, to make decisions, solve problems, relate to people on a pretty close basis. . . . He knows how to be flexible, adaptable . . . But if the college graduate is not oriented to think of what he has to offer, and if the employer is oriented to disqualifying people because of bad attitude or [their lack of] a sense of direction, then the phenomenon of overqualification rises to the surface."

Job-Hunting Problem: Overqualification

Jan Schley, a counselor with Les Gals, a Cleveland employment agency, reflects on the term "overqualification," then pulls a resume from a file. "Here's a girl who has a psychology degree and went on to get a master's in public relations. She's 27 years old, married, types 60 words a minute. To utilize this education I normally go to advertising and public-relations firms. This isn't what she wants. By the time she gets this much education she is so ready to go out and do the boss' job that it isn't even funny.

"Three different interviews she's gone out on she came back and said: 'Jan, in two weeks I would be climbing the wall because I know when I've interviewed with this man that I know more than he does already. It would be total frustration.' And the typical employer would say: 'Wait a minute, I don't want her; she'd overwhelm me.' He doesn't want that constant day-by-day competition."

Many companies lose nearly half of their college graduates during the first four or five years of employment, a trio of industrial experts found. Dr. Marvin D. Dunnette, Dr. Richard D. Arvey, and Dr. Paul A. Banas, reporting in Personnel, an American Management Association publication, spelled out the reasons:

"Only salary levels came close to meeting expectations. Apparently the discontent with opportunities to use abilities spilled over to engender feelings of little accomplishment, boredom with the work, and little hope for advancing upward in the organization."

"Overqualified" is a barrier not restricted to young job hunters. Says Ralph Schepens, veteran Cleveland employment-agency owner and president of the National Employment Association:

"It's a problem for quite a few people who have been in management, well-paid, and all of a sudden for any reason in the world are suddenly unemployed. Most men for at least 30 days try to be practical and try to get back in the same level of position that they had before. Those jobs are tough to get in times of high unemployment. They start getting desperate, and they will now "accept" a lesser, lower-paying position.

"This is a difficult thing for the employer because the man would accept it to put meat and potatoes on the table and pay bills, but he has suffered a blow to his ego and pride in being reduced, and he will use that job as a base for seeking a job like he had before. The employer feels that he will work at his job, but as soon as he can find something like his former position, he is gone."

So too much experience produces for the middle-aged the same barrier encountered by young applicants who have too much education.

"How many of you have been turned down because you were overqualified?" asked Frank Martineau, president of Forty Plus of Washington, D.C., a job-hunting cooperative for middle-aged professionals, at a meeting. Two-thirds of the members raised their hands. How many, as employers, had rejected job applicants for the same reason? Martineau pursued. Nearly half acknowledged that they had.

With groups such as Forty Plus, overqualification may be more than just an excuse. Members are 40 years and older, have earned a minimum of $15,000 a year, and are seeking new jobs for varied reasons.

But, comments a 55-year-old Chicagoan, a victim of an electronic-data-program conversion by his bank employer: "There are too many of us who are looking for a decent job for which we are qualified, who have no ambitions to become controller, vice president, or president but merely want to become a useful part of the business world and society in general. There is no such thing as overqualification. The term overqualified is nothing more than a polite excuse to say you are too old, or whatever the people have in mind."

How can a job applicant beat the overqualification rap? The consensus: Sell your talents rather than your resume, and be sure that your attitude doesn't reflect the idea that the job you seek is beneath your talents. An attitude of superiority surely will bring rejection.

Says Western Michigan's Furbay: "An applicant has no business going to an employer and saying 'This is what I want.' He must go and say, 'This is what I have to offer you.' The degree is not what he talks about."

Martineau tells his Forty Plus people: "The individual has to convince the employer that this job is really what he wants to do. You've got to convince him that you really want to make a career change." In order to do this selling job, Martineau adds, tailor your resume to bring the plus factors to the top, and slant the resume to a specific employer.

An employment-agency operator puts it more bluntly: "I've told many applicants to eliminate some background from their resumes when applying for a job for which they might be overqualified." Deviating from the usual advice, she also tells some well-groomed female applicants to forget the hat and gloves and sleek coiffure when interviewing for a run-of-the-mill clerical job.

Perhaps it's not just a matter of adapting people to jobs but also jobs to people. Comments Dr. Howard C. Carlson, a General Motors psychologist: "There are rising educational levels and accompanying increases in levels of aspirations and needs. When you are increasing the educational input and the job stays the same, then you could be heading for a problem. On the other hand, there's a lot that can be done in redesigning jobs and systems that allows people to have more of an impact on what they do—more voice and more influence on what they do."

But it's frustrating for a job applicant, well-educated and confident of his abilities, to cope with the rebuffs. Comments a Chicagoan with a Ph.D. in applied physics who has repeatedly lost jobs he wanted because he was overqualified: "If the U.S. economy has developed to the point where highly trained people are unable to move out of employment areas where jobs are scarce into other fields where they can be productive, then extensive training may be an actual liability not worth the risk."

Changing Jobs In Mid-Life

Asteel-blue mountain lake in a Western wilderness. A small plane circles a craggy peak, dips, and skims across the water on pontoons. The pilot digs out a Thermos of coffee, a sandwich, and a fishing rod. An hour later he roars off into the sky—a happy man with a "dream job."

Sam Smith is his pseudonym, and he is chief pilot for a state aeronautics commission. The job lets him satisfy twin passions: flying, and hunting and fishing, passions he'd had neither time nor money for as a desk-bound Army-aviation colonel.

Smith found his job even though he's in his late 40s and personnel men by the score had all but convinced him that his service-acquired skills were "not transferable" to civilian life. Smith is one of more than 2,000 middle-aged men and women who've made successful mid-career changes during the last 15 years with the help of an unorthodox little career-counseling firm in McLean, Va., a Washington, D.C., suburb, that has started to attract national attention.

Crystal Management Services, Inc., teaches its clients to avoid personnel and employment offices, executive-search firms, help-wanted advertisements, writing of resumes, and other standard operating procedures of The Great American Job Hunt. Instead Crystal clients go through a searching self-analysis, decide what they want to accomplish with their lives, put aside fear, and sally forth.

146

"Anyone in middle age who looks for a job through the personnel 'system' ought to have his head examined," exclaims John Crystal, a former Sears, Roebuck executive who heads the counseling firm. "Personnel men were put on this earth primarily to screen you out on the basis of some detail in your resume. Age prejudice in this country is just plain horrible. We tell our clients to think of themselves as intelligence officers in an alien, possibly hostile land."

A sampling of typical "Crystalites":

The Rev. Carl Harris, an Episcopal minister, gave up a comfortable parish in Maryland for an adventurous career as Indochina director of World Vision, Inc., a refugee-relief organization.

John Picarelli, a former nuclear engineer in Albuquerque, N.M., is now a consultant to secondary schools and colleges in Maryland and Virginia.

Jack Barnes, an electronics engineer, now works in health-care management in Albuquerque.

Three former Foreign Service officers are directing, respectively, the international department of a Washington, D.C., bank, a foreign-affairs council in a big Midwestern city, and the foreign-trade department of a state in the East.

Dr. Harold E. Sheppard of the W. E. Upjohn Institute for Employment Research in Washington, D.C., says, "A few of us have been preaching the importance of helpful intervention for mid-career changers for the last 20 years, but Crystal is one of the few people who is doing anything *practical* about the problem."

Crystal's program grew from the angry disillusionment with the personnel system he experienced after World War II. Though he had operated behind German lines as a U. S. Army intelligence officer, spoke seven languages, and had an economics degree from Columbia University, "I was a total flop as a job hunter. The only job I was offered was as a Time magazine researcher for $65 a week, and I said to hell with that.

"I figured that if I could get along behind the enemy lines in Europe, then there was something wrong if I couldn't get along in an employment system that was not *actively* out to do me in."

Crystal's course involves 16 three-hour sessions, on week ends and at night, over a period of about six months. Each client's first assignment is to write a 100-page autobiography.

"This is the key to the program," says Crystal. "It's a method of getting you to talk to yourself on paper, to extract from this dialog a clear realization of your strengths, abilities, skills, talents, and desires.

"The great thing about the autobiography is that it gets these men over their fears," says Crystal. "All these guys are scared when they come in. They've all been brainwashed into thinking their skills aren't 'transferable.'"

A former military man with excellent management background wrote that every week end he escapes to the outdoors, hiking in the woods. "But no one's going to pay me for doing this," he added. "Why not?" said Crystal. Sure enough, the man found a job field-testing outdoor equipment for a manufacturer.

After drawing up specifications for their dream jobs, Crystal clients decide where they want to work. Then they visit the region, not to "job-seek" but to scout the territory and talk with local people about schools, the weather, recreational facilities, and opportunities in their field.

Like all good intelligence agents, they study the employment terrain before they get there and seek out people who can introduce them to the top men in the companies that interest them. Before their appointments they make it their business to find out what problems the companies have, and try to come up with solutions. They discuss their ideas with the company big shots, while making it clear that they are not yet hunting for a job, but only looking the field over. Someone has called these "low stress" interviews because each person can test out the chemistry of the other without being forced to make decisions about employment.

A former State Department officer in his 50s, for example, wanted to get into banking, so he surveyed the Washington, D.C., banking community until he found a bank that needed but didn't yet have facilities for overseas banking transactions. He made an appointment with the president, presented a carefully considered program for providing such a service, and allowed himself, after a suitable show of reluctance, to be hired to set it up.

"One of the problems is that our people are forever being offered jobs before they've completed their surveys and found just exactly what they want," says Crystal. "I guess we're the only counseling outfit in America that stood up and cheered when one of our clients turned down a $35,000 job. Getting a 'job' is nothing. There are more jobs out there than people to fill them."

Crystal's little company has attracted attention in career-development circles at a time when the work ethic is coming under increasing fire and some critics say that pensions and "fringe benefits" serve to lock employes into their jobs.

Says the Upjohn Institute's Sheppard:

"One could make the case for the proposition that our institutions do everything in their power to discourage and make it impossible to facilitate occupational change . . . The original motive of pensions and fringe benefits was to lock the guy in. They tied him to the company so that when other opportunities presented themselves, he couldn't go . . . But what too many companies fail to realize is that to the degree the guy is locked in and dissatisfied, he becomes a less-useful employe . . . "

There are some signs of change, however, and Crystal's company is but one example:

● The State University of New York (SUNY) is revamping its curriculum to offer programs for middle-aged career changers. Dr. Alan Entine, a SUNY academic vice president who directed an earlier, experimental new-careers program at Columbia University, is at work on the SUNY curriculum. "With the decline in enrollment of regular undergraduates there is now greater impetus to do this than ever before," says Entine. "We're reaching out for new markets."

● Legislation now before Congress would set minimum vesting and financing standards for private-pension plans, establish a Federal pension-insurance program, and create mechanisms for making pensions "portable."

● The Social Science Research Council, the Fund for New Priorities, and the American Management Association all have major studies under way on the mid-career change problem.

● Catalyst, a nationwide nonprofit organization formed more than a decade ago to help college-educated women find careers outside the home, reports that it now spends much of its time helping them switch careers.

In this atmosphere, "escape manuals" for mid-career changers are enjoying a boom. Notable among them: *What Color is Your Parachute?* by the Rev. Richard Nelson Bolles, and Episcopal priest in San Francisco; *You,*

Inc., by Peter Weaver; *Changing Careers after 35,* by Dale L. Hiestand; and *Career Satisfaction and Success: A Guide to Job Freedom,* by Bernard Haldane.

But no one in the field underestimates the risk. So, while the Rev. Bolles encourages men and women to make the leap, he sends them forth with Christ's admonition:

"Go your ways; behold, I send you forth as lambs among wolves."

EMPLOYE TRANSFERS have slowed down while a growing number of executives absolutely refuse to move, according to a survey of corporate moving practices by Atlas Van Lines of Evansville, Ind. A poll of 127 corporations shows that only 28.5 per cent of salaried corporate employes can now expect to be transferred at least once every three years. The 1973 poll showed that about 37 per cent could expect such a transfer; the figure was 66.7 per cent in both 1969 and 1970. Nearly a fourth of the companies reported that more and more of their employes refuse intercity transfers no matter what inducements of higher pay and greater authority are offered. More than two-thirds of the companies experienced at least one such refusal.

The Condominium Crunch

WHEN Beatrice and Irving Goodman learned that they would have to buy their one-bedroom apartment in North Miami Beach, Fla., for $25,200 or move out, they were dismayed.

They would have to make a down payment of more than $6,000 and pay $1,000 in closing costs. Instead of a monthly rent of $265, their monthly bill would be $278. And they would have to buy a parking space for $500 although neither drives nor owns a car.

After agonizing, they decided, reluctantly, to buy.

"I would rather have remained a tenant, but we have so many friends here it seemed easier to stay than to move," explains Mrs. Goodman. "But think of having to spend all those dollars we hadn't planned to spend."

The Goodman's plight is not unique. A National Observer survey in California, Florida, New York, Illinois, Texas, Georgia, Michigan, Maryland, and Washington, D.C., showed that growing numbers of tenants are getting notices from their landlords telling them, in effect, to "buy or get out."

It's all part of a rush toward condominiums, buildings in which living units are purchased rather than rented. Not only are more and more condominiums being built in the nation's major metropolitan areas, but existing rental properties are being converted.

Many building owners and tenants view conversion with favor:

Tenants gain by acquiring the economic advantages of homeownership while maintaining the conveniences of apartment living. They no longer have to face periodic rent increases (although their real-estate taxes and maintenance costs may go up). They can deduct mortgage interest and real-estate taxes from their income-tax returns, which often reduces their net outlay for shelter to less than what they paid before in rent. And they build up equity instead of piles of rental receipts.

For building owners, condominium conversions mean sizable profits, usually as much as 20 per cent and frequently higher. Owners generally can make much more by selling units to individuals than by selling the building as a whole to another investor. At the same time, conversion can mean getting rid of landlord headaches. Real-estate specialists attribute much of the current owner interest in condominium conversion to the growing militancy of tenants, combined with the growing profit squeeze owners have faced.

While many tenants like the idea of purchasing their apartment, many more do not. Only between 20 and 30 per cent of the tenants in a converted building usually stay, according to several developers. And the news of a conversion often comes as a rude shock.

"If I tell you you've got to buy or move, I'm causing you a problem," acknowledges a spokesman for Luster-Friedman & Co. in Chicago, which says it is the largest condominium converter in the country. "It's a hassle—just moving is a hassle. We all hate to move. You disrupt somebody's life and they're bound to get mad."

Condominium conversions disrupt the lives of some tenants in a variety of ways:

The elderly probably are the hardest hit. Frequently living on fixed incomes, they may find it difficult to meet the monthly payments, which usually are higher than the rent they paid before. If they're living off savings or interest on investments, tying up capital in a down payment reduces their income. If they've been in the building a long time, chances are that their rent is well below the going rate, and they'll have difficulty finding comparable housing elsewhere at similar rents. But if they move, they'll give up old friends and a place where they expected to live out their lives.

An 87-year-old widow living in a newly converted building in Washington, D.C., for example, was faced with leaving the home she had known for over 20 years. She is luckier than many, since her son found another apartment for her and will help pay the increased rent. "She's upset, though," says her son, "because she likes where she is and she knows all the people. When you get that age, you don't like changes."

She decided against buying, he says, mainly for economic reasons. "She would have had to sign a 30-year mortgage, and that's utter nonsense for a woman in her 80s. Her monthly payments would have been almost twice what she's now paying, and she's have wound up owning part of a 40-year-old building that needs all sorts of work done on it. Many people retire on a small income, and they don't want to put their life savings into buying something they don't want."

Young people face different problems. Carolyn Lopez, a 23 year old secretary living in a garden apartment complex in Beltsville, Md., under conversion to condominiums, says she's upset because she doesn't think she'll be able to find as nice an apartment that she can afford.

"I'm having to look for an older apartment, and I'll

have to give up air conditioning, a pool, garbage disposal
—the whole bit."

"If I were married, I'd probably consider it (purchasing her present apartment). Or if I were making $20,000 a year. But right now, I'm not making enough money, and I'd rather spend the money on a trip."

Mr. and Mrs. W. G. Sentelle, who have four children and live in the same Beltsville complex, think they'll move because "what they're asking is a lot of money to still be living under somebody or over somebody and not have land of your own."

"With kids, you always have to worry about noise— yours and someone else's," says Mrs. Sentelle. "If we're going to own a place, we don't want to have to worry about complaints and complaining. I really don't care to go back to a house, though, because that's a lot of up-keep. But so many apartments these days are going condominium, and how many apartments can you find for a large family like ours?"

Usually tenants faced with the question of buying or moving simply do one or the other. City or state law usually requires approval by a certain percentage of the tenants before a conversion can be started. But if a tenant protests the conversion or its terms the landlord need only wait for his lease to expire and then refuse to renew it. Occasionally, though, tenants fight conversions.

When the North Miami Beach building that Beatrice and Irving Goodman lived in was offered as a condominium, several tenants decided to seek changes in the terms of the purchase and maintenance agreements. According to David Osterer, 65, who led a tenants' organization, the proposed contract was a "legal obscenity." It ran for 100 years and gave the owner control over recreational facilities, future pay-TV rights, and mineral rights, and provided high maintenance fees for unspecified services.

The tenants held off signing while Osterer went to New York and worked out a "softer" contract with the owners.

New York City tenants opposed to conversion face a different situation. There most conversions are to co-operatives rather than condominiums. In a co-operative, residents buy shares in a corporation and own the entire building.

Tenants Against Co-operative Conversion has been fighting conversions for the last few years, says Herbert Nagler, co-chairman of the group. Not only do New York landlords reap windfall profits, charge exorbitant prices, and leave tenants with the problems of the building, he says, but they do it all through a system of minority rule, since only 35 per cent of the tenants must approve a conversion.

Nagler says the tenants' group has prevented landlord-inspired conversion of 35 buildings.

For tenants who choose not to fight and are considering buying condominiums, authorities recommend these guidelines:

● Make sure the legal documents are in order, preferably with the help of a lawyer. Do bylaws go into detail on your rights and responsibilities? Do they spell out to your satisfaction what constitutes individual and common property and what your share of the common expenses will be? Are recreational facilities and parking spaces included in the purchase price, or does the developer hold title?

● Investigate the company handling the conversion. Ask your local real-estate board about its general reputation and its experience handling other conversions.

● Look at other condominium conversions in your area. Compare the price per square foot, other charges, financing arrangements, general conditions, and amenities.

● Check whether the building meets municipal codes on fire protection, plumbing, electricity, and other matters. Standards for owner-occupied buildings often differ from those for rental buildings.

● If the seller does not provide an outside engineer's report on the structure, plumbing, heating and air-conditioning systems, and elevators, join with other tenants to employ an engineering team. Try to deduct the cost from the sale price.

● Keep in mind some of the long-term implications of buying a condominium or co-operative. The type of management the building hires and the attitudes of fellow owners can affect the value of the property in later years. Maintenance costs and real-estate taxes may rise. And property that seems a very good investment today may not seem so good tomorrow.

● Don't be stampeded into buying. Harold A. Lewis, a leading condominium consultant and sales broker in Washington, D.C., cautions:

"Just because you're living in the building, it may not mean you should continue living there. There's a great difference between owning and renting. The neighborhood, apartment size, or price may not be what you want, and a person should not compromise on what he wants."

Solar Heating and Cooling

WHILE you kept the thermostat at 68 degrees during the winter and economized on your power needs, energy was going to waste on your rooftop. On a reasonably bright day, sunlight on the roof carried three times the energy your home consumed.

If cost were no barrier you could heat and power your home on today's sunshine—and a few persons do.

But cost *is* the barrier. Realization of the solar-energy potential is waiting primarily for the technology in being to be mated with industry's production and marketing skills. That will take from 3 to 10 years, depending on which expert you ask.

There are, however, signs of immediate breakthroughs:

Bids have been opened for construction of the world's first solar-heated *and* air-conditioned house.

Four school buildings have started drawing a considerable part of their heat from the sun.

A building for the Massachusetts Audubon Society is under construction at Lincoln, Mass., designed to use solar energy for 75 per cent of its heating.

Congress is pushing to equip 4,000 homes with solar heating and cooling units by 1980 at Government expense.

Two Federal buildings, in Saginaw, Mich., and Manchester, N.H., to be completed by 1975, each will use solar heating systems.

A demonstration house at the University of Delaware is producing both heat and electricity from the sun.

And 70 major corporations are supporting a project to build a solar climate-control industry.

"There are very few things that have to be discovered to make solar energy work," says Dr. Peter E. Glaser, vice president of Arthur D. Little, Inc., the research company doing the industrial study. "The only thing that really is needed is the market place has to be right. My own feeling is that with this Government support, with this industry commitment, in the next three to five years this thing will really get off the ground.

"I won't be satisfied until they can buy [solar heating] at Sears or Montgomery Ward in a package, with instructions, perhaps as an add-on to the existing house," says Glaser.

Space and water heating for both homes and commercial buildings will come first when mass marketing of solar-heating units does begin. From 6 to 25 (even experts in the field are not sure) buildings now use solar heat to some extent. Harry E. Thomason has equipped three houses, including his own, in the Washington, D.C., area. He reports an average supplementary fuel cost of $6.30 over three winters. Dr. George Lof, Colorado State University professor of civil engineering, says about 25 per cent of his household heat in Fort Collins, Colo., has come from a do-it-yourself system installed more than 15 years ago.

Lof, who will supervise construction of a demonstration house in Fort Collins under a $238,000 Federal grant, told a congressional committee last June: "It is not unreasonable to expect dozens, or perhaps hundreds, of solar-heated and solar-cooled buildings by 1976." More recently, surprised at new interest in the field, he said, "Make that 1975."

The basic heating process is relatively unsophisticated. Heat collectors, mounted on the roof, have a black, heat-absorbing surface against which water circulates to pick up the sun's heat and carry it into the building's heating system. The top of the collector is covered with glass or plastic to trap heat in a greenhouse effect and prevent radiation back to the sky. It's inefficient at best, but still capable of providing water temperatures up to 200 degrees. Refinement of absorption surface with optical coatings used on space craft promises greater efficiency.

For overnight operation and in cloudy weather, there's a heat-storage system, usually an insulated tank containing heat-retention materials such as small rocks. Experiments with eutectic salts indicate more compact storage is possible. A conventional heat source provides back-up heat during long cloudy periods.

"It's deceptively simple," says Glaser, "but actually you have to be very sophisticated to use solar energy."

The sophistication is obvious when you turn to conversion of the sun's rays into electricity. This requires an entirely different technology, using photovoltaic cells similar to those developed for space craft. Most are silicon wafers, thinner than a dime, treated to create a small electrical circuit activated by light. By arranging numbers of these wafers in a panel, a usable electrical current is produced that can be used directly or stored in batteries.

When first produced in the early 1950s, photovoltaic cells had only about 1 per cent efficiency. Even those used in the space program rarely performed above 10 per cent. But one scientist, Dr. Joseph Lindmayer, claims to have increased them to 18 per cent, with further gains in sight. Lindmayer and an associate, Peter Varidi, quit their jobs at Comsat Laboratories in 1973 to form the Solarex Corp. in Rockville, Md. Lindmayer says they have succeeded in cutting the cost of solar cells "by a factor of 10" (from $200 or more per watt in space to about $20 per watt peak for ground use).

It's true, adds Lindmayer, that further reductions are necessary, for solarcell electricity still costs 10 times that from fossil fuels.

Nevertheless, Solarex has contracted to build the largest solar electrical generating system yet. As an experimental plant on the McLean, Va., building of Mitre Corp., an engineering research organization sponsored by the Massachusetts Institute of Technology. The solar unit will provide under optimum conditions about one kilowatt of energy, adding up to 1,500 kilowatt hours a year, about one-sixth of an average home's use in the area.

Solarex is among the early arrivals in a field expected to bring a proliferation of companies in coming months. While Solarex continues research and pushes toward the solar age, it is contributing to specialty applications. Solar-powered watches, golf carts, telemetry units, power sources in remote areas—all are now a reality.

In climate-control application, solar space heating is far ahead of solar air conditioning. The Fort Collins demonstration house will be the first practical test of a solar-powered air-conditioning system, based on an old idea. A lithium bromide absorption machine (an adaptation of the old gas refrigerator) will be used because it can be powered by the relatively low temperatures of solar-heated water. Slow growth of solar air-conditioning technology has somewhat hampered heating applications because of the desirability of having a combined heating-cooling package.

Immediate application of solar heating to existing homes is handicapped because of high installation costs. The possibilities are much brighter for the new-home market, where for an estimated $2,000 to $5,000 additional cost it can be built in (assuming a reasonable degree of production). While the original cost would be greater, operating costs would be far less than for oil, gas, or coal-fired systems, so installation costs could be regained.

Dr. James B. Comly, thermal branch manager of General Electric's research and development department, has reservations about solar heat for homes ("we're still looking for the right product"). But he sees hope for a combination of solar energy with the heat pump, basically a reversible air conditioner that puts heat into the house in winter, takes it out in summer.

However, Comly thinks solar heating for commercial buildings "could prove to be economic sooner than you might think." General Electric had one of four contracts awarded by the National Science Foundation for equipping school buildings with solar-heat devices. The company has installed 4,500 square feet of heat collectors on the roof of a junior high school in South Boston, Mass., to supply up to 40 per cent of the school's heating needs.

Other school demonstrations have started at Osseo, Minn.; Warrenton, Va.; and Baltimore to prove the state of the art of solar heating.

These are but a few of the "proof-of-concept" experiments the National Science Foundation is financing to give solar energy a boost. From Federal budget expenditures of about $100,000 a year in the 1960s, the solar-research item jumped to nearly $13 million in 1974 and to $50 million in the 1975 budget.

Legislation also is expanding. The House has overwhelmingly approved a bill for a large-scale demonstration program over the next five years. Under the bill the National Aeronautics and Space Administration would contract for 2,000 solar heating plants and 2,000 combined heating and cooling units, using existing technology. The Department of Housing and Urban Development would supervise their installation in Government-controlled properties and in private homes. The resident would acquire them, cost-free after five years of cooperation.

"The public wants to have something that insulates it against the price rises of fuels," says Glaser. "And solar energy for the first time makes the individual independent of the large central power plant, or the oil distributor, or the pipeline company."

"It's that independence that we prize above all else. We may even be willing to pay a premium for it."

Energy-Saving Homes

THE home of the future is likely to be designed with more of an eye to energy conservation than ever before.

According to some architects, engineers, and builders, the "California-style" house that has become popular in recent years—single-family, detached, with big glass windows and a vaulted ceiling—may fall by the design wayside in the next 5 to 10 years. Instead, there may be a move toward multifamily dwellings, more compact shapes, lower ceilings, and less glass. Less dramatic changes will include tighter door and window seals, more storm doors and storm windows, and greater use of insulation.

The changes will come, say housing experts, because American homes have become energy wasters. Among other things, says a spokesman for Levitt and Sons, Inc., one of the country's largest home builders, houses have gotten too big. "They've become a status thing, designed more for show than practicality, just like cars in the '60s," says Hugh O'Haire, director of consumer affairs. "They've gotten away from the function they were designed for—shelter." O'Haire emphasizes that he is not talking about all homes but primarily about top-of-the-line houses.

Builders have known how to build energy-conserving homes for some time, the experts say; they've just needed an impetus. With fuels now in tight supply and heating costs rising rapidly, the impetus is at hand: Home builders agree that prospective buyers will be looking for more energy value for their money. Some energy-saving features, such as fewer windows, will save money; others will increase costs.

The changes are not likely to be revolutionary. Perhaps the most dramatic changes will be in house type and house shape.

"The day of the single-family detached home may be coming to an end," says Karl G. Pearson, professor of business administration and director of real-estate education at the University of Michigan. "Such homes may be relegated to the very, very affluent buyer in the future." But not only because they're energy-wasters, he adds. "With construction costs soaring, the average American family simply isn't going to be able to afford a detached home of its own."

To fill the void, Pearson and others speculate that builders will be building—and families will be buying—more town houses, duplexes, condominium apartments, and other types of multifamily dwelling. Not only are structures that share a common wall less expensive to build than detached dwellings, but they also are subject to less heat loss.

There also will be more moderate-size, compact homes with low ceilings. Ralph J. Johnson, staff vice president of the National Association of Home Builders Research Foundation, predicts more homes approaching the shape of a square and fewer homes in the shape of an "L," "T," or "H." "The closer you get to the shape of a square," he explains, "the more energy you save."

Prospective home buyers probably also will find fewer homes with those big, beautiful picture windows that bring the outside world inside. Glass, a poor insulator against heat and cold, will be used much more sparingly in the homes of the future, says Johnson.

When windows *are* used, they will be better protected by double glazing or storm sashes. Storm doors will also grow in popularity, and weatherstripping and better framing techniques will reduce air infiltration.

The direction that windows face can affect energy consumption, builders say. If there is a choice, they say, it is better for the long walls of a house—and thus most of its windows—to face north and south, rather than east and west. Usually more important, though, in determining what axis a house is built along are such factors as the lay of the land and the location of streets. Builders find it easier to cut heat gain in the summers by shading windows with overhangs.

Finally, prospective home buyers may expect to find insulation an increasingly important energy-conservation technique. Both more and higher-quality insulation probably will be used.

Some builders already are incorporating design features such as these into new homes. Hugh O'Haire of Levitt, which is based in Lake Success, N.Y., but builds homes all over the country, says the company has begun a "national campaign" to build more energy-conserving homes. Among the items on the "campaign agenda": thicker insulation, the inclusion of storm doors and self-storing storm windows as standard items, tighter quality control over construction to reduce air infiltration, and fewer and smaller windows. In addition, the company has begun to reduce the size of its larger homes and to build more attached housing.

"We're going to be more economical, more functional, in our designs," O'Haire says. "Great glass windows and cathedral ceilings are fine for places like California, but they're awful for the East Coast and the central states. We could build homes like this when energy was cheap, but no longer."

Michael L. Tenzer, an official of the Larwin Group, a California-based homebuilding subsidiary of the CNA Financial Corp., says the company is looking at all its plans with the energy conservation in mind but has made no decisions yet. Tenzer says that there probably will be a "constraint" on larger homes in the future—but more because of the rising construction costs than energy considerations. He also expects to see a trend toward town houses, but again, primarily because of the rising price of land and a move toward the multifamily "way of life."

While design features such as attached units and smaller size may help to discourage the rising trend in home prices, many other energy-conservation features probably will mean higher prices for new homes. Ultimately, though, such features as better insulation and more storm windows should save the homeowners money in fuel bills.

Tools for Home Handymen

Despite energy shortages, power tools are selling faster than ever before.

The rationale for the buying surge: Electrical tools for a home shop are used intermittently and exert no sustained power drain. More important, prices have dropped within reach of more budgets.

But as the prices decline and the sleek and shiny power gadgets become more available, the problem remains of what equipment logically should be included on the home workbench.

The basic choice, of course, must depend on the individual handyman's intentions. Is he content with hanging curtain rods, repairing a screen door, building an occasional shelf? Or does he yearn to embark on more ambitious projects, such as building or rebuilding furniture, adding permanent improvements to his home, or creating decorative objects?

There are several versatile, all-purpose power tools that can be used by those in either category. But when the more sophisticated woodworker becomes involved in dovetails and rabbets and intricate contours, the requirements change.

Ask 10 home handymen what power tool is most essential to their shops and you will get a split vote. But chances are a majority will mention an electric drill, and sales figures confirm that this still is the most popular item. Drills are comparatively inexpensive and they're versatile, offering a variety of accessories to perform such jobs as sanding, grinding, paint stirring, and screw driving.

For years the ¼-inch drill, produced in infinite variety and quality, has been the standard. But in the Christmas gift-buying season the accent was on the ⅜-inch model, which offers more power for the odd jobs. The size refers to the diameter of the largest bit a drill's chuck will accommodate.

Drills for the home workshop ranged from $5 to $50 in 1974 depending on their size and quality. Shoppers should insist on a geared chuck that permits tightening drill bits with a key. Besides comfortable handles, convenient switches, and durable construction, a handyman also might consider models that have a variable-speed feature.

A cutting tool is essential in the shop and the most popular is a jigsaw, often called a saber saw. Normally priced from $10 to $50, these machines give a short-stroke, up-and-down motion to small saw blades. A variety of blades, which will cut wood, metal, or plastic, is available. Jigsaws are especially useful in making intricate or irregular cuts, but they cannot make a straight cut as precisely or quickly as a circular saw. A basic feature to consider in selection is the maximum depth of cut. A lightweight model usually is limited to about 1½ inches in soft wood or ⅛ of an inch in soft metal.

Next in popularity comes a sanding tool. There are two basic types: belt and finishing sanders. The finishing tool, providing a short reciprocating or orbital stroke for a flat sandpaper pad, usually is best-suited for home odd jobs. Prices range from $5 to $50, with the orbital type, equipped with a rotary motor, being the more expensive and durable. For heavy-duty work the belt sander, normally priced from $40 to $150, is the tool. However, with its greater abrasive power it can damage a working surface if the user is inexperienced.

Portable circular saws are indispensable for a man who does extensive woodworking or home-improvement projects. Some handymen give them top priority. For home use they usually run from a 6½-inch blade to about 8¼ inches, and the prices generally fall between $15 and $75. Different makes and models offer a variety of gadgetry for regulating depth of cut, operation at an angle, and operational safety.

For the more sophisticated home craftsman, the radial-arm saw has become the center of the shop. With this tool (which normally falls in the $200 range) you pull the saw blade through material placed on the saw table. The power unit can be tilted, turned, and swung on its mounting to give extensive working freedom.

But it's not for cutting alone that one buys a radial-arm saw: With the proper accessories it can become a jigsaw, band saw, lathe, drill press, sander, or router. These are the features that have converted it from a one-time contractor's tool into a multipurpose home tool.

The portable router also is a popular item for serious do-it-yourselfers. New models are available for $50 or less. With this equipment a woodworker can produce standard molding shapes, cut professional-type joints, and do carving.

Most power tools now come in either externally grounded models (requiring a three-prong electric plug) or double-insulated models, providing satisfactory protection against electric shocks.

When you're considering purchase of a shop tool, it's well to study ampere ratings on the equipment to prevent overloading the house electrical circuits. Heavy-duty tools that draw up to 12 or 13 amperes, for example, should not be plugged into a circuit on which any other appliances are operating. Those requiring from 8 to 10 amperes are all right if not used on a line powering major appliances.

Extension cords for power tools also should be chosen carefully to provide the right flow of current. While an 18-gauge wire cord is ample for light tools, heavier cord may be necessary for tools with high amperage ratings. Using the wrong cord can cut the voltage to such an extent that a tool will not function properly and its motor may be damaged.

In spite of the lower prices, power tools still represent a considerable investment, particularly for the man whose enthusiasm runs hot and cold and may let the workbench collect dust for weeks on end. Therefore, when in doubt about the usefulness of a new type of tool it's often advisable to rent one for a trial before purchase.

Those needing guidance in selection of home power tools may profit from the product-buying experience of the Federal General Services Administration by writing for a pamphlet, "Power Hand Tools," issued as No. 16 in the GSA's Consumer Information Series. Priced at 40 cents, it's available from: Consumer Information, Public Documents Distribution Center, Pueblo, Colo. 81009.

Keeping Checked Out

AUTOMOBILE owners who have long lived in ignorance of the mysteries lying under the hood have added troubles when gasoline is short.

During shortages a motorist can't depend on his service-station attendant to routinely check the engine's vital life systems. Lines at the gas pumps frequently preclude anything but the pumping of fuel during gas-sales hours.

The results of neglect may show up on a cold morning when a battery, its water gone, no longer will start the car. The engine may suffer unnecessary wear or even ruin because the oil level has dropped too low. Or perhaps a fan belt, fraying unnoticed, will give way, stranding the motorist in an inconvenient situation.

The prevention of these miseries is simple. A driver should become acquainted with his car owner's manual and learn to perform basic maintenance checks:

Oil level—Locate the dip stick (if it's elusive, check the manual for location). With the engine stopped, pull it out, wipe it clean, and reinsert to get an accurate reading. If the level is below the "add" mark, buy a quart of oil and fill the crankcase yourself, or drop by a service station after the gas-rush hours are over.

Automatic-transmission fluid—Locate the dipstick and check the fluid level. The manual should tell how to do this; usually the engine should be running and the car located on a level area. If you decide to replenish low fluid yourself, make sure you get the correct type for your car.

Battery—Check frequently to be sure the fluid covers the battery plates. When level is low add distilled water (not tap water). Or, you might want to store mineral-free rain water in a plastic jug for the job.

Radiator—Occasionally check the coolant level (it's easier when the car is cold). Remember that if you add much water in cold weather the system may need an extra shot of antifreeze to ward off trouble. A one-gallon plastic jug in the trunk filled with the proper mixture of water and antifreeze is handy for replenishing radiators. Read the antifreeze label for the mixture that will protect against the lowest temperature likely for your area.

Fan belts—An occasional look to spot fraying or undue slack in the belts may prevent a breakdown.

These maintenance items are just day-to-day precautions. For reliable functioning of the car, periodic service at a good station is a good investment of time and money.

The Octane Mystery

FOR many decades the antiknock quality of gasoline has been expressed in octane numbers.

Two methods of arriving at the numbers have been consistently used by the petroleum and automotive industries: the *research* method for measuring antiknock performance under mild operating conditions of low load and low-to-medium engine speeds; and the *motor* method, which measures antiknock qualities of the same fuel under high load and high engine speeds.

Of the two traditional methods, the research method has been by far the more popular—and the more publicized in advertising—for more than 25 years. It produces a number that usually is eight points higher than the motor method.

In 1973 the Cost of Living Council decided to protect the public from possible misrepresentation and fraud by requiring gasoline retailers to display the octane rating of each type sold. The council did not require posting either the research- or motor-octane numbers. Instead, the council ordered use of an *average* of the two, thus coming up with entirely new numbers. The resulting numbers are lower by four than the research-octane ratings.

This created immediate problems. Most American and many foreign auto engines built since 1971 are designed to operate with 91 research-octane gasoline, which is mentioned in recommendations in car owners' manuals. But many motorists have failed to convert the 91 fig-

174

ure to the corresponding average-octane figure of 87. As a result many have ignored 87-octane pumps and needlessly purchased more expensive gasoline.

Some consumer groups and congressmen have complained that the Cost of Living Council's unusual rating system is providing a bonanza for oil companies through increased sales of more expensive gasoline.

Rep. Glenn Anderson, a California Democrat, recently introduced a bill in the House that would require auto manufacturers to substitute average-octane numbers in owners' manuals for 1975 cars.

But the Public Interest Campaign, a group based in Washington, D.C., that is concerned with automotive air pollution, recently petitioned the Federal Energy Administration (which has taken over supervision of gas-pump octane postings) to mark pumps with research-octane numbers. The agency has thus far resisted the suggestion but says the whole matter is "still under review" pending possible action by yet another Government agency, the Federal Trade Commission, on octane ratings.

Still confused? Well, as a practical matter try to remember that 91 in your 1974 or earlier owner's manual equals about 87 on the pump, 93 equals 89, and 99 equals 95. That should handle conversions for most cars built since 1971.

If you don't like going by the numbers, try the trial-and-error approach and use the lowest-priced gasoline that fuels your engine without causing knock.

Car Costs

EVERY time another mile clicks off on a standard-size 1974 car's odometer, it costs 15.9 cents on the average. For compacts that cost is 12.9 cents, and for subcompacts, 11.2 cents.

These are estimates prepared by the Department of Transportation, in which cost factors such as depreciation, maintenance, fuel, insurance, and taxes are figured in. The study is based on a lot of assumptions, including an average 10-year, 100,000-mile life for the car. And the figures were gathered for just one location, suburban Baltimore.

Over the 10 years, costs are $15,892 for the standard car, or $2,339 more than two years ago. The $12,876 total for compact models is an increase of $2,069 in two years, and the $11,153 total for subcompacts represents an increase of $1,709.

In the study published two years ago, Federal Highway Administration statisticians noted that for the standard-size car, gasoline was the third highest expense item, and fourth highest for compacts and subcompacts. "Gasoline is still one of the best bargains on today's market," they reported in 1972.

The latest study reports a sharp change. Gas and oil costs (including taxes) have become the second-highest item for standard cars, trailing only depreciation. And for the smaller cars, fuel is now the No. 1 expense.

The 10-year bill for the standard cars includes these items: about $4,200 to purchase the car, $4,032 for about

7,700 gallons of gasoline, $3,521 for maintenance, $1,618 for insurance, and $1,690 for garaging, parking and tolls.

Figured per mile, the standard car is estimated to cost 4.2 cents to write off the original cost through depreciation, 3.4 cents for maintenance, 3.2 cents for gas and oil (excluding taxes), 2.0 cents for parking, 1.6 cents for insurance, and 1.5 cents for taxes.

The compact: depreciation 2.9 cents, maintenance 2.7 cents, fuel 2.6 cents, parking 2.0 cents, insurance 1.5 cents, and taxes 1.2 cents.

For the subcompact: depreciation 2.3 cents, maintenance 2.5 cents, fuel 2.0 cents, parking 2.0 cents, insurance 1.5 cents, and taxes 0.9 cents.

Check That Deadly
Auto Exhaust

THE exhaust system of your car is particularly susceptible to corrosion damage during the cold winter months. So the signs of spring could also indicate that deadly, odorless, colorless carbon monoxide is leaking under the car.

If as little as about one-half of 1 per cent of the air in a car is replaced by leaking carbon monoxide, death can result within 30 minutes. Far smaller quantites can produce headaches and other discomfort.

The chances of exhaust-system damage and gas leakage are greater if your car is more than two years old. The odds increase even more if you drive extensively in slow traffic or go to drive-in movies and keep the engine idling so the car heater will work.

The muffler and the tail pipe in the exhaust system often don't run hot enough in winter to clear condensing moisture from the engine. You see some of that moisture as "cold breath" coming from the tail pipe on a frigid or humid day. What stays inside damages the metal.

The tail pipe is designed to carry toxic gases to the side or behind a car where they can safely be released. The tail pipe is the last unit in the exhaust system. To guard against carbon-monoxide poisoning, a complete inspection of the exhaust system is essential if a car has been through two or more winters.

You can do it—or have it done—in 10 minutes. It's easier and quicker if the car is on a garage lift.

Start at the manifold at the side of the engine where the exhaust pipe is connected (V-8 and V-6 engines have two exhaust pipes, right and left). Follow each pipe to the first bend, the first likely place for a leak. With a hammer or wrench, pound lightly on any suspicious rust or mud spot to uncover a leak.

Check the joint where a pipe enters a muffler to see that it is sound. Then feel the muffler on its sides, top, and bottom. If there's a rust hole you'll probably be able to stick a finger through the thin metal.

All sections of the pipe to the rear of the muffler are considered tail pipe, although there may be one or two small mufflerlike resonators. The parts toward the rear— farthest from the engine—are the most likely to suffer rust and impact damage because they run at cooler temperatures and stay wet much of the time. Check these parts carefully, especially at bends and turns, and make sure an end piece has not been crimped or partially bent closed by curb impact.

A final check: Run the car engine at idle and try to seal off the end of the tail pipe with a large rag or handful of paper towels. It should be almost impossible to do so. But if you can plug the tail pipe easily and the engine continues to run there's almost certainly a sizable leak in the exhaust system and you'd better check it again.

Auto-Repair Complaint Centers

IF you bought a new car, had it in the shop at least once a week in the first three months, and still had poor gasoline mileage and annoying problems with the choke and transmission, what would you do?

Louis M. Martin of Bridgeport, Conn., called the Automotive Consumer Action Panel (AUTOCAP) for Connecticut. In a few says he had a call from his auto dealer, wanting to make an appointment to deal with his problems.

"I had a feeling he had been pulling my leg before," says Martin. But this time when he left his car with the dealer for two days, things happened. "I still had some problems," says Martin, "but at least through AUTOCAP somebody did something about it."

The same approach might not work for you. It depends where you live. AUTOCAP, a plan developed in 1973 by the National Automobile Dealers Association with the encouragement of Virginia Knauer, special assistant to the President for consumer affairs, is operating in less than 20 areas.

AUTOCAP is a channel for auto owners, frustrated by poor service, shoddy workmanship, or broken promises, to get the attention of new-car dealers and have their complaints arbitrated. "Service is the Achilles' heel of the automobile industry," Mrs. Knauer told a recent meeting of dealers. "Every month complaints about automobiles head the list of problems that consumers write to me about."

Connecticut is a good example of how AUTOCAP can work, although it's too early to get a final reading on effectiveness of the system. Formed in 1973 by the Connecticut Automotive Trades Association, the agency already has received nearly 400 phoned complaints from auto owners.

The process is this: From anywhere in the state an unhappy owner can call a toll-free number and register his complaint. He is immediately mailed a form on which to detail his problem. When the form is returned to AUTO-CAP headquarters in West Hartford, the dealer involved is notified by mail and urged to work out the problem with the customer. If this fails the matter goes before AUTO-CAP for arbitration. The panel consists of four dealers and three public members.

It's the panel's job to arrive at a just settlement when dealer and customer can't agree. Why the preponderance of dealers on the panel? "We have to have credibility with our own members," says Richard D. Meek, manager of the sponsoring dealers group.

"We were very leery about it [the dealer majority] at the beginning," explains John J. Wanchek, a panel member whose Connecticut Citizen Action group is a spinoff from the Ralph Nader organization. "But I have been satisfied with the resolution of every case. There has not been a 4-to-3 vote."

The panel is not a court of last resort. It has no enforcement powers and relies on dealer co-operation to handle complaints satisfactorily. But dealer co-operation has been excellent, says Richard D. Wagner of Simsbury, a dealer and panel head. Only two dealers have balked, one preferring to handle complaints himself and the other rejecting the AUTOCAP idea completely.

When the going gets sticky on a matter of warranty or

car performance, AUTOCAP goes directly to factory representatives. Each time, the manager reports, the manufacturer has been co-operative.

If customers feel they didn't get fair treatment at AUTOCAP's hands, they still can go to the state motor-vehicle agency or take legal action.

"I can only think of two cases where we definitely told the consumer there is nothing we can do for him," says Wagner.

The bulk of complaints deal with service and warranty problems: "I had three transmissions put in this [1974] car and now am waiting for the fourth," complained one owner.

One owner complained of a trunk leak that was discovered after the warranty period had expired and caused a spare wheel to rust. The ruling: "It appears to the panel that the customer has a valid complaint."

Wanchek, satisfied as he is with the progress, has one reservation: "It's a Band-Aid approach, handling only individual complaints. A dealer could do the same thing 100 times and only 5 persons might complain, so he gets away with the other 95."

Where to Complain

• The following auto dealer organizations are operating AUTOCAPs under National Automobile Dealers Association sponsorship:

Kentucky Automobile Dealers Association, P.O. Box 498, Frankfort 40601.

Metropolitan Denver Automobile Dealers Association, 70 West 6th Ave., Denver, 80122.

Automotive Trade Association of National Capital Area, 8401 Connecticut Ave., Chevy Chase, Md. 20015.

Central Florida Dealer Association, 1350 Orange Ave., Winter Park, Fla. 32789.

Idaho Automobile Dealers Association, 2230 Main St., Boise 83706.

Greater Louisville Automobile Dealers Association, 332 W. Broadway, Louisville 40202.

Cleveland Automobile Dealers Association, 310 Lakeside Ave., West, Cleveland 44113.

Oklahoma Automobile Dealers Association, 1601 City National Bank Tower, Oklahoma City 73102.

Oregon Automobile Dealers Association, P.O. Box 14460, Portland 97214.

Utah Automobile Dealers Association, Newhouse Hotel, Salt Lake City 84101.

Louisiana Automobile Dealers Association, 201 Lafayette St., Baton Rouge 70821.

Indianapolis Automobile Trade Association, 822 North Illinois, Indianapolis 46204.

Connecticut Automotive Trades Association, 18 N. Main St., West Hartford 06103.

IF YOU'RE ANGRY over auto-repair delays, here's a word of explanation. The Motor Vehicle Manufacturers Association reports that in the past 20 years, the motor-vehicle population has climbed by about 100 per cent while the number of mechanics increased by only about 30 per cent.

Knitting with Machines

IF your patience is as short as the knitted yarn dangling from your wobbly knitting needles, you may be glad to learn that home knitting has been mechanized, and that machines are increasingly available in the United States.

Manufacturers of the home machines are quick to point out the product looks hand-knit rather than lockstitch knit as is usually produced on industrial machines. Speedy production rather than appearance is said to be the big difference between items knitted on home machines and those laboriously created with hand-held needles. Even a novice can finish a dress in one day, promise demonstrators at the Brother International Corp. in New York City.

Brother is the largest company attempting to persuade Americans to drop their needles, though not their stitches, and to use machines. The Japanese company, which also manufactures sewing machines, sells knitting machines around the world, with its largest markets in Japan and Europe.

Passap of Switzerland, which manufactures a more expensive machine that can double knit, also has established broad distribution in the United States. And several smaller companies, including Genie, Swiss Magic, and Studio, sell models in this country.

Knitting machines have been sold here for about 20

years, but only since 1972 have several models and comprehensive instruction become available.

"This is a multimillion-dollar industry still in its infancy in the U.S.," says Mrs. Ruth Erlich, Brother executive vice president, who predicts knitting machines will someday be as common as typewriters in American households. Brother sales total about 50,000 a year in the United States and Canada; sales in Japan total about 50,000 a month.

Mrs. Sherren Leigh, spokesman for A. C. Weber, the company that distributes Passap machines in the United States, says marketing surveys show that "machine" is still a dirty word among knitters. "They tend to look at a knitting machine as an intruder, not as a creative outlet," she says. "Actually it can enhance creativity. Machines take the doldrums out of knitting, freeing the knitter to create designs instead of endless stitches."

Brother demonstrators emphasize that a person can knit on the machine with the speed of a hundred hands, even though the mechanism is not driven by a motor. Only Passap makes an optional electric drive. Most machines are powered by the knitter, who pushes a flat unit called the carriage back and forth across a bed of needles, with the same sort of motion used in ironing. It's easy to knit up to 200 stitches per second, completing a row with each stroke of the carriage.

Manufacturers emphasize that even old persons who suffer from arthritis can use a knitting machine because no finger work is required.

Although all the knitting machines are basically manual devices, some are designed to produce automatically a pattern or certain type of stitch. Brother has four models, ranging from a manual machine to a model that utilizes computerlike punch cards to produce certain results by automatically controlling the configuration of the needles.

Passap has only one model, the Duomatic, which has a double bed of needles and controls tension without weights. Passap says these features offer greater versatility and a less stiff knitted product. Brother sells a ribbing attachment to achieve double bed knitting on some of its models.

A knitting machine can handle all types of yarn up to four-ply worsted, including cotton yarn and even string. Manufacturers provide special patterns, but a person also can make up patterns and adapt hand-knitting patterns. Most models can produce multicolored and Argyle patterns and lace and woven effects. The Passap machine crochets.

Goods knitted on a machine are so like hand knits a person can stop the machine and use hand-held needles to finish a garment with no visible difference, manufacturers say. Like the hand knitter, the machine knitter must block and sew the pieces together to finish a garment.

Brother personnel insist that the machine is easily mastered, even by those who previously used yarn only to tie up a package or a pigtail. But the mechanism itself isn't simple, and it would be difficult to progress quickly beyond the pot-holder stage on your own.

Before a single stitch can be made, would-be knitters must assemble such equipment as Sinker plate unit; a holding-cam lever, and the right and left extension rail fasteners. There are numerous buttons, knobs, and dials. Lack of formal instruction for beginners has slowed sales, but Brother and Passap both report progress in overcoming this problem. Passap is attempting to ensure that each sales person in its 500 U. S. outlets can knit a complete garment. Knitting lessons are mandatory, even for appliance-store owners who aren't used to learning how to cook before selling a stove.

Brother offers a 12-lesson correspondence course free with the purchase of a machine. With the institution of the course, Brother believes it has cleared the big hurdle and is stepping up distribution. Currently it has about 1,500 outlets in the United States and Canada and is pushing for inclusion in mail-order catalogs.

The Passap distributor has begun to emphasize knitting machine rentals as well as sales. "A person who knows she doesn't want to knit enough to make the purchase price worth-while can rent a machine and make a few special items," says Mrs. Leigh. "If the person decides she wants to keep the machine, some of the rental will apply to the sale price."

She says not all dealers have begun to rent machines although all are now encouraged to do so. Many already rent machines to institutions such as public schools, vocational training centers, and homes for the handicapped.

Mrs. Erlich believes the knitting machine has a basic appeal to men as well as women because of its mechanical aspects. And she believes its popularity abroad will spread to the United States. Word has already reached the Soviet Union, she says. When the Russian Philharmonic appeared in New York City in 1972, two members of the symphony bought machines to take back. And she says nearly 30 Turkish sailors have bought machines: "They come in when their ship gets to New York."

But family purchases are expected to be the mainstay of the knitting-machine market. "If children outgrow a sweater or tear a hole in it, you can unravel it and knit it over in short order on the machine; you couldn't do that by hand," says Mrs. Erlich. "Yarn lasts nearly forever. When a woman gets tired of a dress she can just reknit it in a different style, using the same yarn. I know one woman who keeps reknitting only a few dresses. Everyone thinks she has a terrific wardrobe."

Knowing the Tennis Racket

MORE than 1½ million Americans will be bitten by the tennis bug in 1974. It produces a powerfully addicting disease that incubates in the winter months, begins to spread in springtime, and reaches epidemic proportions in summer. Most of those newcomers to the game, along with many of the 15 million Americans who already are addicted, become utterly confused when they begin shopping for their first racket.

As tennis has boomed in this country—the number of players has doubled in the past five years—so has the tennis-racket industry. Only a few years ago a player could choose from half-a-dozen generally similar wood rackets. Now a player must choose from dozens.

"One of the biggest problems facing the consumer," says Wilson Sporting Goods executive Tim Healy, "is understanding the plethora of rackets on the market. Often he decides solely on the basis of price and cosmetics—the best-guess system."

But given the soaring price of rackets, the best-guess system can be costly. Tex Schwab, executive director of the United States Professional Tennis Association, believes the most common error among first-time racket buyers is extravagance. "The public seems to want the most expensive racket, which is not necessarily the best racket," says Schwab. "And often it's not the best racket for them." The solution? If you're buying your first tennis racket it probably will be worth the few extra dollars a professional may charge to profit from his or her advice. "A professional," Schwab says, "will take into account your budget, your size, your shape, and your strength before recommending a racket."

If a tennis pro isn't available in your area, look for a shop that specializes in tennis or sporting-goods equipment and keep asking questions until you find a salesperson who can answer them. But before you start asking, reconcile yourself to the fact that a good, durable racket that will last a minimum of two or three seasons will cost at least $20 in 1974 dollars. On the plus side, however, a tournament-level racket that will last indefinitely need not cost much more than $20.

One guiding principle in buying a racket, whether from a pro or a discount house, whether your first or your 50th, is *feel*. Find a racket that simply feels comfortable in your hand and is well balanced. While you're testing for feel, incidentally, don't limit yourself to a "man's" or a "woman's" racket. The differences between the two are purely cosmetic. Wilson's Billie Jean King Autograph model, for example, is identical to the Stan Smith Autograph model, save for the decals. Most women's rackets, however, are available in lighter weights and smaller handle sizes than most men's rackets; the most popular racket for women is 4½ light, and 4⅝ medium for men.

Still another guiding principle: Don't be inordinately swayed by player endorsements. Just because Pancho advertises Brand X doesn't mean it's the right racket for you. In fact, it might not be the right racket for him. When Rod Laver won the U. S. professional indoor title in Philadelphia recently he did so with a wood racket. But for the picture-taking ceremony he slipped over it a cover emblazoned with the name of the metal-racket maker whose product he endorses.

Now you're ready to decide whether you prefer wood or metal. Since 1967, when Wilson introduced its steel T-2000 model, metal rackets have been the rage and their number and variety is now staggering, not to say bewildering. Generally, the advantage of metal is that an average player can swing it faster and thus hit the ball harder. The disadvantage, be well advised, is that the inexperienced player just may spray the ball all over the court. What you gain in power with a metal racket you may lose in control. And manufacturers' claims to the contrary, metal rackets can and do break.

Without pretending to be an exhaustive survey of all the reputable rackets available, here is a brief primer on the characteristics and prices of the leading rackets. And to defer to fashion, let's begin with metal:

Wilson's steel T-2000 was the first widely popular metal racket. It is extraordinarily flexible—"whippy," the pros say—and is set apart from all other metal rackets by its trampoline design: the strings are not attached directly to the frame but to a spidery metal guidework that's attached to the head. This results in a slingshot effect in which the tennis ball is almost caught in the strings and flung back. The Wilson T-3000, introduced in 1972, is essentially the same racket but for a steel wedge at the racket throat, which prevents the racket head from twisting under pressure and gives the player more control. While most tennis specialty shops and sporting-goods stores sell the T-2000 and T-3000 frames for about $33 and $38 respectively, they can be purchased at discount houses for prices beginning in the mid-$20s, already strung with good-quality nylon.

Head, renowned for its skis, started making tennis rackets in 1969 and now carries four models whose devotees call them the best metal rackets available. The

Knowing the Tennis Racket

Head Standard costs about $40 prestrung with high-grade nylon while the Master model comes without strings for about $35. There is scant difference between the two, both of which play like a sensitive and yet fairly stiff wood racket. The Head Professional model features a tear-drop shaped head, very stiff playing character, and a heady $47 price; it is not a racket for beginners. Head's Arthur Ashe Competition model is probably the most exotic racket on the market and, at $55, one of the most expensive. Resembling a graceful rug beater with its open-throat design, the Competition consists of a fiberglass frame sandwiched between high-tensile aluminum; there have been instances of the lamination coming apart and warpage. "This is a racket for serious tennis players, the advanced player who has his game under control," says Head's Jim Lilstrom. "It combines power and touch."

Spaulding encountered numerous problems with its initial aluminum racket, the Smasher III, but the company now says it's licked them with a redesigned model. "But it's a heavy racket," says Tom Morgan of the Tennis Shop in Washington, D.C. "The medium feels almost like a heavy and so it eliminates the racket for most women." The $35 price tag for the frame alone may also eliminate it.

Basically there are two kinds of wood rackets: flexible and stiff. A quick rule of thumb for telling them apart: Examine the shaft; the thicker the shaft and throat, the stiffer the racket. Conversely, the narrower the shaft and throat, the more flexible the racket.

The most flexible and perhaps the most attractive wood rackets are made by Davis, whose rackets also carry the initials TAD. "We usually steer women toward the Davis frames," says Morgan, "because they're more flexible." One popular model among beginners and experts alike is the Imperial ($22 unstrung), while the Imperial Deluxe ($27) is slightly stiffer because of an extra overlay of wood on the shaft and throat. Davis' Classic I may be the whippiest wood racket around, while the Classic II is slightly stiffer; both carry a $40 price tag, unstrung.

British-made rackets include the Dunlop Fort, which is one of the most popular frames made and, at $21, a very good buy. "The Fort, however, is notorious for breaking," notes Morgan. "But people who are devoted to them don't really care." Another British-made racket is the Slazenger Challenger No. 1, a nondescript looking, stiff-playing racket for the strong, serious player ($27 unstrung).

"Bancroft makes good rackets," says Tex Schwab, "but they've got a hell of a lot to choose from." Make it simple and consider Bancroft's three basic frames: the Player Special ($23.50), the Super Winner ($25), and the Bancroft Executive ($28.50). They are, in the same order, stiff, fairly flexible, and very flexible. One nice feature about Bancroft rackets is their rectangular handle, which allows a player to know quickly where his hand is on the racket handle, an important plus for beginners.

The most important thing to remember about Wilson wood rackets is that they are extremely well made and, in the autograph series, almost identical. The differences between them are subtle—the difference between, say, a Pauillac and a Saint Emilion. Both are Bordeaux wines, but each has its special flavor. So, too, with the Wilson woods, which cost between $22 and $25 for the autograph-series frames. The subtlest of them is the Jack Kramer Pro Staff model.

The best buy for a beginner? Perhaps the Davis Hi-Point model, which is generally available prestrung with high-quality nylon for $19.95. It is an attractive, durable, and flexible wood racket.

Knowing the Tennis Racket

In the final analysis, of course, whichever racket you choose will suit you best if you believe it does. "More than half the problem in selecting the right racket is above the shoulders," comments John Conroy, for more than a quarter-century the tennis coach at Princeton University. "Besides," Conroy adds, "the better player is going to win no matter what kind of racket he uses." True enough, but what kind of racket does John Conroy use? Wood one day, metal the next. Different folks have different strokes.

Cut-Rate Encyclopedias

FEW people sit around all day reading encyclopedias from aardvark to zither. But Larry Teacher of Philadelphia spends much of his time studying encyclopedias because he promises his customers detailed comparisons and lots of advice on the sets sold in his unusual store.

Teacher's Discount Encyclopedia Center is one of a very few stores where you can walk in and browse through encyclopedias as you would examine other books. There are two similar firms in New York City: Literary Mart and Reference Book Center.

Because the only sets available to such outlets are used, savings are substantial, even though many "used" sets are unwanted and unused gifts or prizes. Cost is usually two-thirds to one-half of the original price. For example, recent editions of Britannica sell for about $250; a new edition costs $598 from the publisher. The stores handle only major encyclopedias, including *Britannica, Americana,* and *World Book.*

The encyclopedia stores offer buyers several advantages denied both the classified-ad shopper and the person who purchases from the publishers' door-to-door salesmen.

If you buy a secondhand set from someone without a guarantee, you may later question the bargain when you discover something you're seeking is on a page that has been ripped out. Checking each page yourself could be arduous. But Teacher promises that his merchandise will be intact: no pages missing, no crayon marks obscuring the text, no bindings bitten in two by someone's dog. The New York City and Philadelphia stores also promise to exchange a set for any other encyclopedia stocked if the customer later decides a different set would be better suited for his or her needs. That's true even if the replacement set is less expensive, necessitating a rebate.

The opportunity to shop comparatively is a significant advantage, the owners say. "I encourage people to come in and compare how subjects are treated in the different sets. I tell them to bring in their children and let them read from several sets," says Teacher. Even mail-order or phone shoppers benefit by receiving comparative information on several sets at once. In fact, Teacher insists his objectivity is more important to many families than the discount price.

Regardless of the outlet chosen, the American Library Association has some valuable consumer guides on buying encyclopedias. Its magazine, Booklist, contains reviews of numerous encyclopedias with approval or disapproval clearly stated. To obtain a list of issues containing specific reviews and reprints of articles on buying a general encyclopedia, a child's encyclopedia, or supplements, write the ALA Reference and Subscription Books Review Committee, 50 E. Huron St., Chicago 60611.

The encyclopedia stores also welcome inquiries. Consumers may write Discount Encyclopedia Center, 38 S. 19th St., Philadelphia 19103; Literary Mart, 1261 Broadway, New York City 10001; and Reference Book Center, 175 Fifth Ave., New York City 10010.

Buying Antiques

AN upholstered buggy seat, a Sheraton four-drawer chest, a steam-driven clock, a mechanical cast-iron bank, a 1940 TV set, a brass bed warmer, a Louis XIV chair, a Hepplewhite sideboard, a cuspidor, a cranberry scoop, a Coolidge campaign poster, a silver napkin ring, a Betty lamp, a fancy painted chair, a biscuit tin, and a cigar-store Indian.

These are a few of the thousands of kinds of old merchandise that are the stock-in-trade of the nation's antiques industry, an industry that is now experiencing its greatest boom ever. Prices are soaring, many once-abundant items are becoming scarce, and fakery and misrepresentation are on the upswing.

"Never before has it been so important for antiques hunters to know the true value of the pieces for sale in shops and shows," says Ralph Kovel, who with his wife, Terry, is one of the nation's best-known writers and lecturers on antiques.

"It's not that antique dealers are less honest than other businessmen," adds Kovel. "On the contrary, the ethical level in the trade has traditionally been high. But the antiques boom has brought a lot of amateur dealers into the market, and many of these dealers don't know much about what they're selling."

Ralph Kovel was not referring to museum-quality antiques that are bought and sold by experts. Such pieces are relatively easy to identify and their value is well established.

But most people who go hunting for antiques are not prepared to pay thousands of dollars for an Eighteenth Century Philadelphia highboy or a Louis XIV chair. Most antiques buyers are operating on middle-class budgets and are looking for early Nineteenth Century country furniture, mid-Victorian furniture, china, glass, silver, and miscellaneous old artifacts that are viewed as interesting decorator items.

The biggest single factor in the soaring prices of such articles is the enthusiasm of many young marrieds who are furnishing their first homes. These buyers, with their limited budgets, combine a distaste for new "plastic" furnishings with a desire to recapture something of the past—especially since many old pieces remain bargains.

Says Jim Stocker, an auctioneer at A-B Auctions in Portland, Ore.: "Kids are buying old furniture because they have gotten beat so bad on modern stuff. Take beds. Buy a new one and it falls apart in three years. But an old one of tough wood like oak and the craftsmanship of the earlier days gives kids a solid piece of furniture they can refinish and redo to their heart's content."

A check by National Observer correspondents throughout the country shows dealers to be in general agreement about the shape of their industry. They say that prices are climbing fast (although they disagree about how fast), that young people coming into the market are a major factor, that there is a severe shortage of pre-1830 furniture, that more and more fakes—especially in glassware—are popping up, and that the advent of the bank credit card has made it easier for more middle-income people to buy the antiques dealer's wares.

There is another factor too, say Ralph and Terry Kovel, whose best-selling *Know Your Antiques* is considered by many the best primer in the field. Declares Terry: "A lot of cash goes into antiques to *hide* cash. A fellow could easily put $25,000 into a couple of good pieces and, when the tax man comes by, the explanation is that the pieces belonged to his father."

The Antique Dealer, a trade journal, estimates the industry's annual volume is $700 million. But just what is an antique?

The U. S. Government, for customs purposes (there is no import duty on antiques), recently changed its definition from any item made prior to 1830 to any item now at least 100 years old. Nevertheless some dealers, like E. R. Wilkerson, Inc., in Atlanta, remain purists. Says Wilkerson: "My firm is only interested in antiques produced before 1830," when handmade furniture gave way to machine-made pieces.

The Kovels, who publish annual price guides for the industry, say that as a practical matter there must be other definitions of "antique." One popular, if somewhat facetious, definition is "anything that's sold in an antique shop." Adds Ralph Kovel: "An antique can also be something that's the oldest of its class. For instance, I have a 1940 two-inch TV set. That is certainly an antique."

If an item becomes a fad, the price will go up regardless of when it was made. One hot item is brass beds, which first were made early in this century.

Says auctioneer Luster Douglas of Louisville: "I'll be darned, but some teen-agers have $500 to pay for a brass bed."

Henry Chilton, another Louisville auctioneer, remarks: "Used to be you could get a brass bed in Montgomery Ward's for about $16. Now a 'rough' one costs $150 to $200 and a polished brass bed can bring up to $600."

Another popular item is the old icebox, which young people are buying for about $125. "A few years ago you couldn't give those things away," muses one dealer. Buyers are using iceboxes as stereo cabinets and bars.

Mrs. Sara Simonsgaard, a dealer near the University of Chicago, observes: "Right now there is a great demand for old looms, and they are relatively difficult to supply. The people who buy them actually use them to weave."

Terry Kovel declares that some of the best buys now are in 1880-era furniture. "The demand for this later Victorian furniture hasn't developed yet, but it will. There are still plenty of bargains available in this ornate furniture, partly because there's so much of it around. We can be sure the prices will go up."

The price rises that have already occurred, just in the past few years, have been spectacular: Several dealers say flatly that an antique bought 10 years ago has doubled in value.

Paul Schumann, a dealer in Louisville for 42 years, says prices on American antique furniture have gone up 150 per cent in the past decade, with increases in the past two or three years of up to 25 per cent annually.

Ralph Kovel says that average antique prices climb 10 per cent a year. "That's why so many more people are getting interested in antiques," he adds. "They are a good investment. If you buy new furniture all you have when you get it home is used furniture that's worth a fraction of the price you paid. Antiques rarely go down in price, except for certain items that may fall out of fashion."

Says J.H. Elliot, Jr., of J. H. Elliot Antiques in Atlanta: "The prices are going up because antiques are increasingly scarce . . . I think the scarcest items are dining chairs. This does lead to fraud. We've always had it in this business. The other day a woman from Alabama came by to show me a set of pearl-handled knives which she bought as antiques. She said the blades were supposed to be new but the handles were supposed to be antique. The entire set was new and I told her to take it back where she bought it. That sort of thing gives all of us a bad name."

Frank Sullivan, a dealer in New Market, Md., a village of 300 people and 31 antique shops, says that dining chairs, even though scarce, are not always a practical buy. "Chairs made 200 years ago were made for people who were smaller all around than we are today. And they were lower. The height can be made up by using casters, but there's not much you can do if the chair has a too-small seat."

Price and variety often vary regionally. Regions that were settled later, such as the Far West, generally have fewer old American pieces around. Says Robert M. Kasper, a prominent San Francisco dealer: "In the West, as far as I can determine, there is no interest in quality American antiques. I don't know any big dealer who specializes in them. The demand is for English, not American, antiques."

When good American antiques do appear in the West, the prices are almost always higher than in the East. Reeder Butterfield, a San Francisco auctioneer, reports he has an Eighteenth Century maple highboy that he expects will bring $15,000. A similar highboy sold just 22 months earlier for $9,000.

That, of course, is not the kind of piece the average

American buys. Most people are buying country furniture (that is, furniture made by rural craftsmen, often using such famous "city" styles as Hepplewhite and Sheraton). The only country furniture that commands very high prices today are pieces made in the 1600s—the Pilgrim century—and these items are extremely rare.

The common quest is for late Seventeenth and early Eighteenth Century pieces such as desks, chests of drawers, dry sinks, tables, and hutches. Usually refinished in natural wood tones, these pieces generally cost hundreds of dollars. They're cheaper "in the rough" but the buyer must be prepared to tackle the job of stripping them.

Better buys are usually available at shops with low overhead—in other words the country store. Frank Sullivan of New Market, Md., says it's possible for him to sell antiques much cheaper there than if his shop were located in Washington, D.C.'s Georgetown or another high-rent neighborhood.

Nor must antiques dealers even have a store. Many dealers sell strictly through antiques shows, which have multiplied until even many small cities always have an antiques show in progress.

Where do experts such as the Kovels buy their antiques? "One of the best places," says Terry, "is at house sales. When people are selling the entire contents of a house they often are content to take less for an antique than what it is worth."

"Auctions are also good places to buy," adds Ralph. "But make sure you get there early so you have a chance to examine the items. Then decide the maximum amount you would pay, and stick to it. Don't get carried away."

To decide what you should pay for an antique, it's first necessary to know the going price. Much to the chagrin of some antiques dealers, more and more antiques hunters are buying the Kovels' annually updated book, *The Complete Antiques Price List*. It lists prices for 40,000 antiques, based on dealer transactions throughout the country.

Many people who already own antiques would like to know their present worth. Although most appraisers charge several hundred dollars or base their fee on 1 per cent of the items' value, many dealers will appraise antiques for considerably less.

Veteran buyers and sellers of antiques contend that ethical conduct has generally characterized the field. They point out that many dealers stand ready to take back any item sold and refund the purchase price or apply it toward a more expensive item.

But as the antiques business has expanded, as antiques have become scarcer, and as many more amateurs have entered the market place, the temptation to misrepresent pieces and even to fake them has increased. Nor is the fakery always subtle. Twenty miles northeast of Atlanta on the Buford Highway is a roadside sign proclaiming: "Antiques—Factory Outlet."

To help avoid the risk of antique buying, the Kovels compiled this list of 10 caveats for National Observer readers:

● You can only buy a bargain if you know more than the dealer. Study.

● Beware of reproductions, especially glass, the easiest antique to copy.

● Beware of the never-was "antique" that was made for today's gift shop. Ash trays of early styles of glass, milk glass, Mason jars, and cast-iron miniatures are just a few of the pseudoantiques found at many shops.

● When buying furniture, be careful not to get a

piece that is married (two unrelated pieces joined together, such as a table and a high-boy top), glorified (extra carbing added), or a reproduction.

● Ignore the family history of historic-personage associations. Believe only verified documents attesting to ownership and history.

● Check for repairs, breaks, repaints, and missing parts. A black light will show many of these.

● Watch out for phony labels and signatures. Faked signatures etched into glass and paper-makers' labels are becoming more common.

● If you fall in love with an antique you don't know about, pay what a similar new piece would be worth to you. You can never overspend if you consider the use only.

● Watch out for fads. At times certain types of antiques are in top demand, commanding top prices. Then the fad fades, and the antique's value fades with it.

● Remember that antiques do not improve with age. If it wasn't pretty when it was new, it never will be.

Little Old Winemaker You

WHEN Richard O'Neill moved into a new house at Camp Hill, Pa., he debated whether to devote a large, dark area under the garage to wine making or mushroom growing. Wine making won out and now the business executive is turning out wine right at the annual 200-gallon maximum the Government permits a family for personal use.

Dr. William McCall of Harrisburg, Pa., a gynecologist and obstetrician, chose wine making when he was looking for something to do when he was on call and had to be near his home phone every third night.

R. Dixon Herman, judge for the U. S. Middle District in Pennsylvania, responded five or six years ago to advertisements pushing the joys of wine making and now turns out "pretty good wine at [a cost of] 25 to 50 cents a bottle." He's partial to locally grown blue grapes, which he crushes with a potato masher.

Not since Prohibition—which gave rise to the Federal laws governing wine making for personal use—have so many persons become enamored of the fermented grape. Some have gotten into wine making, convinced that they can turn out a product superior to commercial wine. O'Neill, for example, is a serious oenologist who keeps detailed records and can trace back every processing step taken with every bottle of wine.

The hobby is so popular that many stores stock winemaking materials and there are even franchised stores dealing exclusively in wine making. Jack E. Cooper, president of a company that supplies wine makers through six stores in Pennsylvania and New Jersey, estimates that amateur wine making is growing even faster than the booming commercial wine industry.

Cooper was among 125 persons attending a Wine Conference sponsored by Pennsylvania State University, the Pennsylvania Department of Agriculture, and the Pennsylvania Grape Council. Cooper was among suppliers worrying with the happy problem of how to keep up with demand.

Cooper's stores are among 120 nationwide that are affiliated with the Wine Art Corp. of California, a major supplier of concentrates and equipment. Cooper's annual sales have gone in three years from $100,000 to more than $500,000.

Paul Scotzin teaches wine making at a supply store he and his brother operate in Lemoyne, Pa. He insists that wine making is no more complicated than mixing orange juice if grape concentrates are used. The concentrates range widely in cost from about $10 to $40 in 1974 dollars a gallon, with each gallon making about five gallons of wine.

After the concentrate is mixed, it is allowed to stand for about a week and then is shifted to a jug with a valve that lets the gases of fermentation escape without admitting air. After a month or so, clear wine is racked or poured off. The container is cleaned and the wine is returned for another two months or so and is then racked again. The clear wine then goes back into the cleaned jug for a few days and can then be drunk.

"Beginners will make wine and drink it at the end of the three months," says Scotzin. "But it gets better the longer you keep it. By making subsequent batches, bottling that, and putting it away, you can accumulate a cellar full of wine."

For Harold A. Swenson of Harrisburg, a major charm of wine making is that it's not too demanding. "It's not like you've got to feed the goldfish or they die," he says. "You never have to say, 'Well, next Saturday I must do my wine; if I don't do it, it gets better and I'll do it the following Saturday.'"

Swenson spends an evening about every three weeks on his hobby. Unlike Judge Herman, he says "there's no way I can make a quart of wine for less than a dollar." Even though he may not be saving money, however, Swenson says "I have an awful lot of fun making my own wine."

John Healey, a Bell Telephone engineer in Harrisburg, is among the wine hobbyists who believe they do save money. Volume may help keep his costs down. Healey says he once made wine in one-gallon lots but now his minimum is five gallons. He explains that it takes no longer to process five gallons and if a batch turns out particularly well, he has a much longer-lasting supply.

The novice can get into wine making for $25 or less. But it isn't hard to spend more money on equipment and supplies. Dr. McCall made an initial investment of $150, though he concedes he got into wine making on "a pretty big scale." He says a wine maker who uses fresh grapes and other fruits in the summer could run his annual bill for expendable supplies to from $150 to $200.

O'Neill, the AMP, Inc., executive who chose wine over mushrooms, is in wine making in a big way. He's had his own labels printed up and developed his own filtering system (plus his own process for making champagne, which he says costs him about 25 cents a bottle). O'Neill even had a chemist make him up a wax and plastic seal for the necks of his bottles.

And like most amateur wine makers, O'Neill particularly enjoys having friends in to sample his wines. "I had 30-some people in the other week for sampling wines and champagnes . . . You get recognition from this and I guess we all enjoy being a specialist at something."

Motorcycling Saving and Pitfalls

THERE'S the ignition, this is the clutch, down there is the gearshift, and here is the gas feed and brake."

My instruction complete, I lurched down the deserted street (after stalling a couple of times) and joined the great motorcycle boom.

Surviving the experience I can understand (1) why people are turning in unprecedented numbers to powered bikes for utilitarian purposes, and (2) why so many riders wind up as accident statistics.

Not that there was any real element of danger in my trial jaunt. It was the equivalent of Junior shoving off on his first bicycle ride—with trainer wheels. None of this leaping over the crest of a hill, or roaring down the highway. For me, and for a large slice of today's bike buyers, that remains fantasy.

In growing numbers people are joining the putt-putting parade, using comparatively low-powered bikes for errands, commuting, and as a general substitute for a second car. A street bike adequate for these chores generally costs from $800 to $1,200. Economy and convenience are the keys.

"Dealers all over the country are reporting substantial increases in the [age] 35 and up customer who has never ridden a cycle before," reports the Motorcycle Industry Council, "and whose first question is, 'How many miles will I get to the gallon?'" (Answer: At least 40 to 50, with makers of some new models claiming 90.)

About 85 per cent of the motorcycles sold in December 1973 were lightweight street bikes. And that month's sales figures brought the total registration of motorcycles to an estimated 4,222,000, or five times the figure of 10 years ago.

The cycle activity is strongest in California, where about 15 per cent (630,000) are registered. Michigan is a distant second with 262,000 registrations.

Dealers throughout the country reported a record bike demand in the spring of 1974, with many selling the lightweight models as fast as they arrived in the showrooms. Japanese manufacturers, who provide the bulk of the street bikes, are having raw material shortages and can't keep up with the demand.

The surge of sales is not without its problems for motorcycle makers and the general public. Inexperienced riders are venturing out onto crowded highways and creating new traffic hazards. Nearly 3,000 cyclists died in accidents in 1972 and the National Safety Council estimates more than 300,000 were injured.

While safety statisticians figure cyclists are three times as likely to be involved in fatal or injury-producing accidents as auto drivers, they don't automatically blame the bike riders. It's the interaction of two-wheeled and four-wheeled vehicles that produces the danger. A University of North Carolina study found that in 62 per cent of accidents between cycles and cars, the auto driver was at fault. The common reason: "I just didn't see him."

New laws attest to the motorcycle traffic and safety problem. Nearly all states require cyclists to wear helmets. More than half require a special license, periodic safety inspections, and eye protection. About one-fifth require use of the headlight, day and night, so the vehicle will be more noticeable.

But most licensing tests are easy and don't qualify the operator for daily use. "Most state licensing tests are a joke," says Lewis S. Buchanan, safety specialist with the National Highway Traffic Safety Administration. "They're a balancing exercise, not a driving test."

Indeed, many officials aren't convinced motorcycle operation requires any great skill. "It's just like riding a bicycle," commented one Maryland safety official.

But the Motorcycle Safety Foundation believes driver instruction is the key to improving the safety record. (One study shows three out of four cyclists in accidents had received no instruction.) Organized by the six major cycle manufacturers, the foundation is attempting to bring motorcycle-rider instruction up to a par with auto-driver education in the public schools. Eight workshops in 1973 trained college instructors, who in turn will train highschool teachers. This year the goal is for 40 workshops.

Though more than 2.5 million highschool students are taught to drive cars each year, motorcycle-rider instruction was reported in only 107 schools in 1973.

Motorcycle enthusiasts agree that few bike dealers provide anything but the most rudimentary instruction for customers. "Why should they?" one asks. "When did you get any driver training from an auto dealer?" A few private schools for motorcycle instruction are now cropping up to meet the need.

So the preriding instruction I received corresponded with that most bike buyers get. And my instinctive reactions to the riding experience must have been roughly those of any novice who has rarely been on a bicycle since childhood.

As I wobbled down the street, one statistic crossed my mind: An accident survey indicated 20 per cent of the riders were using a cycle for the first or second time. And the person who borrowed a bike was nine times as likely to have an accident as an owner.

But I had little time to think of statistics. I had a feeling of isolation, locked inside the bulky helmet and peering out through a plastic visor. Using the controls was like the child's exercise of rubbing one's head while patting the stomach. Exhilarating it was, even at 10 m.p.h. And the straightaways were pure pleasure. But when it came to reversing the course, some subconscious force always seemed to twist the throttle when I intended to brake, or prompted me to squeeze the clutch when acceleration would have been more appropriate.

I hoped there was no one home at the residence where I jumped the curb and traversed the lawn in a futile attempt to negotiate a smooth turn. And I marveled at the calm attitude of the bike owner as he watched my erratic course.

Venture out in traffic? No way. I was confident that with an hour or two of experimentation I could handle the vehicle well—if nothing got in the way. And it was a relief to settle into the familiar surroundings of my car.

I have resolved to give a wide berth to the next motorcycle I encounter on the highway.

Novice motorcycle riders and teachers looking for instructional materials can obtain a comprehensive textbook, *The Beginning Rider Course,* by sending $1 to: Motorcycle Safety Foundation, Inc., Publication Service, 1001 Connecticut Ave. N.W., Washington, D.C. 20036.

Family Coats of Arms

A gaunt greyhound carrying the leg of a chair in its mouth is dominant on the coat of arms that Henry Fleisher received.

"I think my wife wondered what kind of family she had married into when the picture of that greyhound arrived," says Fleisher. The Washington, D.C., advertising executive says he ordered the report on his surname and a copy of what he understood to be the family coat of arms because a direct-mail advertising letter intrigued him.

"After all, it was only a couple of bucks," says Fleisher. "Considering some of the lousy shows and movies I have seen for much more money, I'm not sure that the amusement derived from all of this hasn't been a pretty good entertainment bargain!"

Though Fleisher regards his $2 rendition of the greyhound as a joke, many serious genealogists aren't laughing. They contend that many buyers of mail-order heraldry are getting coats of arms to which, by the unenforceable rules of heraldry, they aren't entitled.

Nor are the genealogists mollified by the disclaimers in most advertisements that say something like, "No genealogical representation intended or implied."

And the mail-order genealogists rub salt in the wounds of the traditionalists by frequently peddling such accessories as wooden wall shields at from $9 to

$20, pewter tankards at $35, statues of knights at $14.50, and large plaques for $75.

Genealogist Richard E. Coe of Beverly Hills, Calif., calls the mail-order companies "opportunists" who take advantage of the general lack of knowledge about heraldry. Coe, who is herald of the National Genealogical Society, contends that most persons who order coats of arms by mail assume that what they will receive is a reproduction of a symbol used by their ancestors. That's very unlikely, says Coe.

Coe says that with rare exception there is no such thing as a coat of arms for all families with a given surname. The arms design was granted to a particular individual, and by the ancient rules of heraldry, only his direct descendants are entitled to display that coat of arms.

"Using one of these so-called family coats of arms is like hanging up an old portrait of somebody else's ancestor and claiming him for your own," says Coe.

Because coats of arms were granted to individuals, rather than to families, there are often many different arms registered to persons of the same surname. There are, for example, 67 different coats of arms for the name Lewis and 88 for the name Ward in one reference book. That explains why two different mail order companies sent different coats of arms to a reporter. For a fee of $4.95, the Sanson Institute of Heraldry in Boston mailed a sheet of paper with a decal in the form of a shield bearing three gold cinquefoils and a stripe across the middle. A parchment family tree chart, an essay on the development of surnames, and a map of Europe in 1097 was included too.

For $2, Halbert's, Inc., of Bath, Ohio, sent a parchment-like print of a shield bearing two silver chevrons and three silver shells. This coat of arms is complete with the crest, or helmet ornament, which consists of a smug-looking greyhound who appears much better fed than the skinny animal depicted on Henry Fleisher's coat of arms. Halbert's inserted a history of surnames as well.

Cadlyn's, Inc., a Long Island company, sends the first coat of arms registered for an individual with the surname of the person placing the order. If the customer specifies more information about his ancestry, the Cain president says, the company might send another coat of arms associated with that surname.

Coe notes that in England, where coats of arms are regarded as property, it's illegal to use symbols a person does not own. A registry of all coats of arms is main-tained by members of the College of Arms, who are ap-pointed by the British monarch. The college also grants new coats of arms to persons of academic and profes-sional distinction.

Residents of the United States may be able to obtain a coat of arms officially recognized by the College of Arms in one of two ways:

If the applicant can trace his ancestry back to a British subject entitled to a coat of arms, the college will do the necessary research to verify the claim and will send a copy to the American applicant. For a minimum fee of $45, the college will determine if the British emigrant ancestor had a right to use a coat of arms. But the fee is higher if the applicant has no information about the key emigrant ancestor, according to Mrs. Frank Collins, Jr., of the National Society of Colonial Dames XVII Century, a genealogical society headquartered in Washington, D.C.

If the United States resident discovers his British ancestor had no coat of arms, he can apply to the college for new arms to be issued in his own name, providing he can establish his own distinction in some field.

The cost of arms in either instance depends on the hours of research required. Mrs. Collins says the rate is $15 a generation. Expenses may run about $400 or more.

Mrs. Collins emphasized that ethnic origins do not disqualify an applicant as long as he can trace his lineage to someone who lived under British rule. Therefore, many Americans must trace their lineage back to the end of the Revolutionary War—1783. She says inquiries may be sent to the College of Arms, Queen Victoria St., London, E.C., 4, which will send an estimate of the cost of obtaining coats of arms.

Coe suggests a simpler way to get one's own coat of arms: Have someone familiar with heraldry design a coat of arms; then the cost is mainly for the actual art work.

One company neatly ducks the problem of matching up coats of arms with descendants of original recipients; it offers prints of old ships that it says brought bearers of various names to the United States. Homes-Corey, Ltd. of Marco, Fla., charges $8.95 for a print for names on an advertised list of 256 names. There's an extra charge of $3.95 for names not on the list.

Or you can just forget yourself and order a coat of arms for your dog. Several companies are advertising coats of arms designed for 11 breeds of pedigreed dogs, with the head of the "ideal" subject in the center of the shield.

Slow Cookers

THE latest group of kitchen appliances for slow cooking makes it possible to produce inexpensive but nutritious meals without using up a lot of the cook's or the nation's energy.

The electric slow cooker originated with the Crock-Pot, a Rival Manufacturing Co. product. The Kansas City company introduced the concept and has the most widely distributed line of cookers. But it now has competition from some 18 manufacturers.

Preparing food in a slow cooker requires much less heating energy than use of a conventional gas or electric stove. Rival home economists say they have cooked five-pound pot roasts in two ordinary ovens and in a Crock-Pot. During the 10-hour cooking time, the Crock-Pot used 0.75 kilowatt hours of electricity. A well-insulated, self-cleaning oven used 2.73 kilowatt hours during four hours of operation, and a regular oven used 4.59 kilowatt hours.

The new units save human energy because the cooking process requires little or no supervision. Once the food is in the pot, it can safely be left to cook for 10 to 12 hours. Timing isn't crucial, so the electric pot is ideal for a person who wants a home-cooked meal waiting upon returning home from work.

The cookers consist of a covered crockery or glass casserole dish surrounded by or set on a heating element, which maintains a steady temperature of 200 or

300 degrees. More expensive models have pots that can be removed for washing. Suggested retail prices of the various types ranged in 1974 from about $18 to $40.

Slow cooking in a sealed pot helps food retain natural juices so it's less likely to dry out or overcook than if cooked conventionally. Mrs. Kay Rambo of Loveland, Colo., says that a slow cooker helps her battle inflation. "I discovered that my Crock-Pot makes any cut of meat tender, juicy, and good to eat," she says.

For those who want more recipes adaptable to slow-cookers, Rival offers *McCall's Book of Wonderful One-Dish Meals* accompanied by a leaflet on conversion to slow cookers. Send a check or money order for $2.95 to Customer Services, Rival Manufacturing Co., Box 19556, Kansas City, Mo. 64141.

Aluminum Keys

MANY persons use aluminum-alloy duplicates of original keys for doors, cars, or what-have-you because they are lighter and more easily colored for identification than regular keys. But colored-aluminum keys can cause more trouble than ordinary keys.

A woman in Washington, D.C., opened the bolt lock on her apartment door with a blue key and started to turn a red key in a second lock. The key snapped. A locksmith's bill for removing a six-month-old aluminum key: $14.

The red key had been made by a clerk in a department store. The customer would have had trouble buying the same type of key at a professional locksmith's shop; many locksmiths won't use aluminum because they say it breaks more quickly than the more conventional brass alloy or sometimes nickel-silver alloy used for keys.

Manufacturers of aluminum key blanks defend their product. A spokesman for Cole National Corp., a major maker of aluminum-alloy key blanks, says independent laboratory tests show the tensile strength of aluminum keys to be equal to or greater than brass keys. Locksmiths, in his view, are disgruntled by losing business to department-store key duplicators.

But tensile strength isn't everything, say some anti-aluminum locksmiths. They say that the cut or irregular side of an aluminum key is sharper than the corresponding side of a brass key and is more likely to chip or flake or to scar lock tumblers. Then, they say, the key begins to turn roughly. Eventually it resists turning, cracks, and finally breaks.

An executive of the Independent Lock Co., which makes both aluminum and brass keys, agrees both that aluminum keys do well in strength tests and that they break more often than brass keys.

Whatever the key metal, locksmiths offer these tips on lock maintenance:

Keep the lock clean. Dirt and grit can make tumblers sluggish (and easily picked). Squirt some lighter fluid into the lock every now and then and run the key in and out. If it still doesn't work smoothly, squirt some powdered graphite into the lock after the fluid has had a day to dry. Never use oil on a lock; it fouls the mechanism.

Keep keys clean because they can carry dirt into a lock.

Occasionally inspect keys—especially car keys—for signs of wear. A key that doesn't slide smoothly into a lock is generally ready for replacement.

Buying Batteries

RUNNING to the corner store for batteries has become almost as much a part of the post-Christmas scene as taking down the Christmas tree. More and more toys, games, electrical appliances, tools, and communications devices run on batteries, and frequently the batteries in new merchandise fizzle out quickly.

Once the consumer gets to the store, however, he may be confronted by a bewildering variety of batteries or, alternatively, may find only one or two general-purpose types, while what he needs is a special-purpose battery.

Even after the consumer has narrowed his selection to those that satisfy the voltage and current demands of his equipment, he still may need to know, for example, whether a carbon-zinc or an alkaline battery is better suited to his needs. Different battery types are better for different purposes, and the consumer would do well to be aware of the characteristics that differentiate one type from another.

Basically, there are five kinds of "dry-cell" batteries on the market (as opposed to the "wet-cell" lead-acid battery used in automobiles and other heavy equipment): the carbon-zinc, alkaline-manganese, mercury-oxide, silver-oxide, and nickel-cadmium.

The carbon-zinc cell, the typical "flashlight" battery,

comes in a variety of shapes and sizes and is the cheapest, most widely used, and most readily available. It comes in two types—the lower-priced or "standard" and the higher-priced or "premium" models. Most manufacturers indicate that the premium models last as much as twice as long as the standard models, and several independent studies show that the premium often measures up to that claim. The premium may also cost up to twice as much.

Carbon-zinc cells usually are sold as general-purpose batteries and can be used in radios, flashlights, toys, photoflash guns, tape recorders, and a variety of other devices. But you may get better service from carbon-zinc cells designed for special purposes, as, for example, a "transistor" carbon-zinc cell for transistor radios.

The carbon-zinc battery works best when only a light current is needed and the usage is intermittent. Alkaline-manganese, or alkaline batteries, as they're commonly called, are more suitable when greater energy is needed and the usage is continuous.

The alkalines are billed as "longer-lasting," and since they are usually interchangeable with the carbon-zincs, many stores recommend them for the same general-purpose uses. But the alkalines are also more expensive, so the consumer must determine whether he's going to get his money's worth. Generally, that depends on the specific use intended for the battery.

A study by Consumers Union indicates that alkaline cells last about a third longer than premium carbon-zinc cells for intermittent usage, as with a flashlight. But since the alkalines usually cost between two and three times as much, they're a questionable bargain in that sort of application.

On the other hand, the same study shows that alkaline cells offer two or three times the service life of premium carbon-zinc cells with high-drainage usage, as in toys, and several experts say that's true whether the usage is intermittent or sustained. In some usages, manufacturers contend, the alkalines may provide 5 to 10 times the service life of the carbon-zincs. But at least one manufacturer's representative says the life may be nearer 1½ to 2 times as much.

Where the usage is heavy and continuous, however, most experts agree that the alkaline cells come out at least as good as the carbon-zincs on a cost-per-watt-hour basis, and better as the current needs increase. And since replacement is needed less frequently, the alkalines hold a convenience edge.

Other advantages of alkaline cells over carbon-zincs include their longer shelf or storage life and better performance in low temperatures. They're also considered superior when a large amount of energy is needed quickly, as with photo-flash equipment.

Most dry-cell batteries are not designed for recharging; once the battery is "dead," it should be replaced. The alkalines, though, are available in both nonrechargeable ("primary") and rechargeable ("secondary") types. The rechargeables cost about twice as much as the regular alkalines but can be recharged several times.

Mercury-oxide cells provide more energy with less weight and bulk than any other. In addition, their high-temperature performance is excellent. For these reasons, they come into their own as miniaturized batteries used in heart pacemakers implanted in the body, hearing aids, and electric watches.

Mercury-oxide batteries can also be used for radios,

photo equipment, and transistor devices, but here the question of cost enters. Mercury batteries are about twice as expensive as alkaline cells and four to five times as costly as standard carbon-zincs. Their service life is equivalently greater, however, so they need to be replaced less often.

Silver-oxide batteries supply slightly higher operating voltages than mercury-oxide batteries. They provide good low-temperature performance and, like mercury-oxides, are used in miniature form for hearing aids, watches, and other small devices. The silver-oxides are generally about the same price as the mercury-oxides, but because of their different voltage characteristics, the two are not usually interchangeable.

The most expensive dry-cell battery is the nickel cadmium. As a high-quality, rechargeable battery, it is enjoying increasing popularity as the power source for portable hand tools, portable appliances such as electric shavers and movie cameras, and communications, equipment such as long-distance radios and walkie-talkies. Besides its recharging capacity, features include good high- and low-temperature performance and ability to provide both high-power bursts of short duration and steady power of long duration.

Some nickel-cadmium-powered devices, such as electric toothbrushes, can be recharged simply by plugging them into a wall socket. Other items must be recharged using a special recharger, which sells for about $6 to $10. If you don't want to bother with this, or if the battery finally does wear out, you must usually return the entire item to a dealer to get a nickel-cadmium replacement. It's difficult to buy battery replacements in exactly the right size and shape on the open market.

If the differences between battery types still leave

you confused, you're not alone. The American National Standards Institute, which draws up voluntary standards for industry, has recognized the general confusion and established a committee to draw up a system for grading batteries by use.

The secretary of the committee, says that when selecting a battery, the buyer should consider five factors:

Will it give the longest life for the use you intend?

Is it reliable—that is, ready to use when needed?

Is it resistant to leakage, especially when a switch is left on?

How often must it be replaced, and what is it worth to you to avoid a trip to the store?

Does it work well in the weather you'll be using it in?

Some additional pointers on the purchase and use of batteries:

● If battery testers are available, test batteries before you buy. Many batteries sold as new have actually been kept on the shelf for some time and at temperatures higher than the recommended maximum of 70 degrees.

● To store batteries at home if you buy several at once, put them in your refrigerator in a plastic bag. If you buy in bulk and for use over several years, store the batteries in a freezer.

● Once a battery loses its power, don't keep it in the appliance. The battery may leak, releasing a corrosive ooze that can not only destroy your appliance but can also be dangerous to your own mucous membranes. And be wary of batteries advertised as "leakproof." None is completely leakproof, and the Federal Trade Commission has forbidden advertising any as such.

● If one battery in a series goes bad, it's a good idea to replace all of them. The others are likely to be on the verge of going bad and may run down the new battery.

Buying Batteries

● Unless the battery specifically states that it is rechargeable, be careful of recharging. Not only does the possibility of battery leakage increase, but some batteries may explode. Recharged batteries, unless designed for recharging, usually don't last long anyway.

Smell Selling

SMELLS sell. They sell laundry detergent, shampoo, used cars, dish-washing liquid, disposable diapers, lingerie, cleaning compounds, bath oil, deodorants, shaving cream, cleansers, hair sprays, cosmetics.

It is no accident that clothes laundered in Tide smell the way one might expect freshly laundered clothes to smell; Tide contains an ingredient whose sole function is to impart the smell to clean clothes. Without a similar ingredient, Pampers disposable diapers wouldn't smell like much of anything; with it they smell like babies, or at least as many people imagine babies ought to smell.

Used-car dealers sometimes spray a car's interior with an aerosol to make the car smell distinctively "new."

Two displays of identical women's hosiery were placed on a counter. In one display the stockings were lightly scented; the rest were not. Most women chose the scented stockings. Ditto brassieres.

Product fragrances are created by a small, anonymous group of people called perfumers. A perfumer can develop an elegant new perfume for women, put fresh fruit in a can of shaving cream, or plant a mountain forest in a bottle of floor cleaner.

The perfumer's tools are several thousand known fragrances. Some are exotic: galbanum from Iran and Lebanon, oak moss from Czechoslovakia, opopanax from the Middle East. Others are merely unusual: Castorium is extracted from the testes of beavers. A perfumer's laboratory may contain as many as 55 variants of a fragrance such as jasmine or rose.

The great perfumers consider themselves artists and describe their work in the language of music and painting. A fine perfume has a top note, a middle note, and an end note, and may require the subtle blending of several hundred chemicals.

"Each perfume has a characteristic fragrance," says Harry Cutler, a perfumer for Florasynth, Inc. Cutler, who has been creating fragrances for perfumes for over 30 years, says that when creating a new fragrance a perfumer might "take a known fragrance and give it a new twist."

"If I took Chanel No. 5," he says, "and gave it a honey-tabac-jasmine character, I would produce something shocking. It'd be the difference between night and day. Is it an entirely new fragrance? I don't really know," says Cutler. "You can't create in a vacuum. You have to have something to base your work on."

What accounts for our attraction to pleasant scents? No one knows, really. Science does not fully understand the mechanism of the human nose, whose ability to detect nuance in odor is 1,000 times greater than the most refined techniques of chemistry. Yet it is said that the nose's sensitivity to smell is but a fraction of what it was when man relied on his senses for survival.

Advertisers and marketers of fragranced products wish they knew more about the olfactory mechanism and the way odors affect man. Researchers are investigating the possibility that odors may alter our moods, in the way colors have been found to affect mood. Others are looking into pheromones, chemical substances thought to sexually attract insects and animals to each other across great distances. Fragrance companies feel that if men and women give off subliminal, sexually attractive odors, and if they can synthesize these odors—well, you can imagine.

Until then the merchants of smell must settle for, say, the Schick Shaving Experience, or "SSE," a transcendent something one apparently feels when shaving with Schick's new "herbal-forest" or "fresh-orange" shaving creams. Such aggressive odorousness in products is, with some exceptions, a fairly recent phenomenon. Indeed, the people who manufacture fragrances sometimes call their product "the secret salesman." The smell of pine has successfully and without fanfare sold cleaning compounds for decades.

Now the salesmen are shouting their secrets. An advertisement for Clairol shampoo says: "It all begins as soon as you open the bottle and breathe in the breathtaking, close-to-the-earth essence of forest herbs and mountain flowers inside Clairol herbal essence shampoo. Juniper, birch leaves, Cinchona, Melissa, Mountain gentian . . . The whole experience does beautiful things inside of your head, too. And it is an experience. The most beautiful shampoo experience on earth."

Some market observers contend Proctor & Gamble started the direct appeal to our noses when it put lemons in Joy dish detergent. Since then manufacturers have squeezed lemons and limes into everything from cosmetics to Janitor In A Drum in the belief that citrus connotes something clean and fresh.

"Clean and fresh!" That's the message manufacturers hope their scented products will waft to the customer's brain. Why? Because so much else now is rundown and dirty. "The aim today is not to have anything unpleasant in life," says Stuart Hinrichs of International

Flavors and Fragrances, Inc., a company specializing in the development of new flavors and scents.

The feeling is that modern man and woman endure a foul, filthy world. Cars fill the air with "the old Detroit perfume," says songwriter Paul Simon. Drinking water smells strongly of chemicals. The Atlantic Ocean is awash in plastic. Nature is defiled or done in.

Advertisers and marketers quickly saw the solution to this polluted existence: Package a purified nature and sell it. Splashing and sprouting in the aisles of any large supermarket one may find a shampoo "with the essences of 11 herbs," a fabric softener that "adds the fresh smell of April to clothes," bath-oil beads fragranced with "twilight mist, garden moonlight, dawn mist, and summer nocturne," Tahitian Lime Scent deodorant, a bathroom ammonia with a "new springtime scent," and other scented products.

Within the text of an advertisement whose headline reads, "A frank discussion about the limitations of bathroom tissue," one finds that Wet Ones moist towelettes have a "pleasant, fresh scent."

Honeywell has developed an odor "counteractant" called Scentrol, a device to be installed in the ductwork of a central-heating system or mounted on a wall. It masks undesirable odors with four alternatives: mint, orange blossom, cinnamon and spice, and mountain air. "The system can also be turned off," says Honeywell, "so you can enjoy such pleasant odors as holiday cooking."

Some of the perfumers' creations for the new "natural" products do indeed contain natural essences, though these substances generally cost more than synthetically produced fragrances. And sometimes natural isn't natural enough: Most lemon-scented products are fragranced synthetically because natural lemon doesn't smell enough like lemon to most people.

People once were content merely to kill off odors that bothered them. The best smell was no smell. Now "people are looking for products that do something to them, that give them a strong experience," says Dr. J. Stephan Jellinek of Sensory Signals, Inc. Laundry detergents can't just clean clothes; they have to *smell* like they've cleaned the clothes. In a test, women who washed clothes with the same detergent—one scented, the other unscented—said the scented laundry was cleaner.

Perfumers generally prefer to talk about creating new perfumes intended for men and women rather than those to be stirred into a detergent or tube of lipstick, says perfumer Cutler. But cosmetics, hair sprays, and household products comprise the bulk of the perfuming business, and correctly matching fragrance to product image is often critical to the product's success.

"If you're making something that's going to be used to wash dishes," Cutler explains, "the fragrance would have to be compatible with food." Hand creams: "If it's going to be a cosmetic hand cream, you can fragrance it, but if it's going to be used in the kitchen, it has to smell differently—citrusy, maybe." Hair sprays: "It can't be overfragranced, or it'll compete with her perfume." Shampoo fragrances "shouldn't last too long."

"Then you have medicated products," Cutler says, "which are expected to smell like medicine. Many products, like creams or soaps that have a specific medicinal use, are deliberately not fragranced to smell nice; they're fragranced to smell horrible," he says. Without such smells, he says, buyers tend to react with, "Gee, if I can't smell it, how good can it be?"

Meet the Metric System

A typical newspaper page measures approximately 2,422 square centimeters. The entire newspaper weighs about 230 grams.

That may do little for you except evoke memories of little-understood conversion tables in the back of an old textbook. But at Western Michigan University in Kalamazoo, the Center for Metric Education is studying ways to make those metric terms familiar to you—or, more precisely, to your children and their teachers. Knowing them will be useful in the next 5 years, essential in 10.

Know them you must, for the United States is going metric. The impetus has come not from Government decree, not by popular demand, but from industrial action keyed to economic necessity. The public is generally unaware of the trend.

One by one the giants of U.S. manufacturing have plunked for metrics: General Motors, Ford, IBM, Caterpillar, Honeywell, General Electric, 3M—the list is growing. They want to market the same products at home and abroad. Since the United States is the lone nonmetric industrial nation, it has become obvious that a change must be made or markets will be lost.

' What will metrics do for the U.S. consumer? Directly, very little. Indirectly, perhpaps quite a lot. Says Dr. John L. Feirer, director of the metric education center: "We're becoming a have-not nation. If we fail to convert to metric standards, we're putting ourselves behind an extra eight ball. Metric conversion can simply mean more jobs for more people." Since the big industrial companies are already well into the use of the metric system, Feirer add, "It's going to be the small guy who is going to suffer from lack of knowledge of metrics."

Once learned, the metric system is actually simpler and more logical than the conglomeration of inches, feet, yards, ounces, pounds, and quarts we've grown up with. We must divide feet by 12 (or yards by 36) to get inches, and pounds by 16 (or quarts by 32) to get ounces, for example.

Much of the metric system, by contrast, is based on a single unit: the meter (39.37 inches). It's a decimal system, meaning it's based on the number 10. Thus the meter is devided by 100 and 1,000 to get centimeters and millimeters, respectively, and multiplied by 1,000 to get kilometers.

And the metric system established a definite relationship between the linear meter and units of weight and volume. A gram is the weight of a cube of water one centimeter on a side. A liter is the volume of a cube 10 centimeter on a side, or 1,000 cubic centimeters.

Eventually you'll buy carpeting by the meter, meat by the gram, and gasoline and milk by the liter. And until consumers learn to think in metric terms, there's little choice but to remember that a meter is about 1.1 yards, a liter is a bit more than a quart, a four-quart gallon contains about 3.8 liters, a kilogram is 2.2 pounds, an ounce is about 28.4 grams, and a kilometer is about 0.62 miles.

The average engineering school lags in use of metrics, says Feirer. "But in five years when an engineering graduate goes out to get a job, one of the first questions he will be asked is, 'Do you know metrics?'"

Even the average job is going to require some metric knowledge. Secretaries, for example, will have to become familiar with the units and their spelling.

There is one other change of terms that will affect everyone: determining the temperature. With the metric system comes a switch to the Celsius (formerly centigrade) scale. On that scale water freezes at 0 degrees, boils at 100. Normal body temperature becomes 37 degrees, and a 25-degree day will be comfortable.

This metric system shouldn't be all that foreign to us. Congress recognized it in 1866 as valid for "contracts, dealings, or court proceedings." Since 1893 the metric measures have served as the basis for all U.S. standards.

But putting it into daily use is something else. From a long history of inches, pounds, and quarts that trickled down from Roman days and involved such arbitrary standards as the size of barleycorns and the girth of a Saxon king, we are so wedded to a familiar system that change seems unthinkable.

It's not that much of a dilemma, says Feirer. Metric conversion as proposed would take effect first in promoting industrial change in machine tools and essential manufacturing components such as screws and bolts, as well as education. Then it would creep into consumer goods.

Geared as we are to governmental guidance, the formal action will come from Congress, which has shown little enthusiasm for a conversion. But two bills are being considered that would establish a metric-conversion board, which would be given a year to establish a plan for coordinated conversion. Then a 10-year conversion period would start, with the goal of voluntarily establishing metrics as the "predominant, although not exclusive" measuring system.

The only significant opposition has come from the AFL-CIO and some small-business spokesmen. And there has been pressure to grant governmental subsidies, either through loans or generous tax write-offs for new tools and machinery needed to meet metric standards.

During the 10-year-conversion period:

↙ Children would be taught metrics. Maryland already has decreed metric education, beginning in September 1974, and California plans to start in 1976. Textbook publishers are grappling with the problems involved.

↙ Gradually, metric terms would come into the market place. In fact, some consumer goods already show contents in both U.S. and metric measures.

↙ As the change-over progresses, products would be marketed in metric sizes, eliminating some of our odd-weight packaging and making price comparisons easier.

Speculation on the program is not all blue-sky thinking. Other countries are pointing the way. In 1965 Great Britain started conversion. The incentive was clear: More and more, England was dependent on trade with metric Europe.

England has done a good job of changing industry and education, says Feirer, who has studied Britain's conversion, but has made little progress in the consumer field. Letters-to-the-editor columns in British papers are heavy with complaints about tinkering with familiar standards. And there are accusations that some merchants are gouging the public by using unfamiliar metric terms.

Others are finding the going smoother. Australia and New Zealand started their shift to metrics in 1970; they're already ahead of England in consumer acceptance. Canada, too, has edged into the metric age, but appears to be dragging its feet to see what the United States will do.

In late 1973 Feirer carried the metric message to educators from the Mississippi Valley, meeting in Chicago. Other workshop sessions in the series reached educators in every section by the end of the school year. Using visual aids, transparencies, and metric tools and kitchen measures, the center's staff shows educators the shape of the teacher's task ahead.

The metric center is a small pilot project, financed by the U.S. Office of Education, seeking to determine the educational problems expected from conversion. While finding teacher educators generally receptive, Feirer recognizes the difficulty of reaching the students. "Most of today's teachers resist change," he observes.

There are a few signs of the change to come. Ford Motor Co.'s Mustang II has the first domestically produced metric engine. A few highway signs show distances in both miles and kilometers. And druggists have abandoned the old apothecary units of drams, scruples, and grains in favor of metric measures.

The National Bureau of Standards, after a three-year study, urged Congress in 1971 to go metric. From soundings of more than 700 national groups, the bureau's researchers reported about 50 per cent believed the change inevitable, desirable, or both. Another 45 per cent indicated it didn't matter, and 5 percent were opposed.

Inevitable it appears, although there is little question that many will cling to old ways, and criticism will abound. One such criticism appeared in the letters column of an Australian publication:

"No doubt many readers have noticed, as I have, that since eggs went metric they have been pale in yolk colour and lacking in freshness. This clearly shows that chooks [chicken] cannot adjust to laying different-size eggs. We tamper with nature at our peril!"

FAULTY ELECTRIC SHAVERS can pose a danger to externally worn heart pacemakers. The problem isn't frequent, but a doctor writing in the Journal of the American Medical Association says that if the shaver isn't running smoothly, its electrical signal could disrupt the pacemaker. An official with the U.S. Food and Drug Administration agrees that the problem occurs rarely, but that a patient with an external pacemaker should test it while using an electric shaver before leaving the hospital. The electric-shave problem rarely, if ever, affects an implanted pacemaker worn internally.

STAIN REMOVAL is explained in "Removing Stains From Fabrics," a Department of Agriculture publication. The booklet tells how to remove 142 common fabric stains. It's available for 20 cents from Consumer Product Information, Pueblo, Colo. 81009. Specify home and garden bulletin number 62.

HADDOCK FANCIERS may have to substitute other fish as haddock becomes even more scarce. The National Marine Fisheries Service says haddock had become "almost commerically extinct" even before the United States and 15 other nations agreed to a near-total ban on further haddock fishing during 1974 in the Georges Bank area off Cape Cod. Fishing boats will be allowed to catch only about 10 per cent of a normal full catch from the waters, which marine experts believe have been depleted of haddock by overfishing or environmental changes.

IF BIRDS or small animals threaten to harvest your fruit and vegetables before you can, consider keeping them away with a garden net rather than with pesticides. Designed to allow normal passage of air, sunlight, and moisture, the lightweight mesh can be safely draped over fruit trees, bushes, and vines. Netting is sold at many nurseries and is also available from Ross Daniels, Inc., Box 430, West Des Moines, Iowa 50265.

'Shots' For Travel

WHENEVER would-be globe-trotters start getting that faraway look in their eyes, it means they've begun to plan their next vacation.

Immunization shots have been a standard part of the getting-ready procedure. But the Government's vaccination requirements are now easier than ever to fulfill.

For a variety or reasons, the U.S. Public Health Service (PHS) has gradually reduced vaccination requirements for persons returning to the United States. The only immunization requirement now for re-entry is that persons who within the preceding 14 days have been in a country reporting smallpox-infected areas must show proof of smallpox immunization.

As recently as 1971, all travelers returning from abroad were required to be vaccinated against smallpox. Cholera and yellow-fever vaccinations were required if travel had included infected areas. But a decline in the world-wide incidence of these diseases, recognition of the limited effectiveness of some vaccines, and occasional untoward side effects have led to the removal of these requirements.

This does not mean that persons going abroad may forget vaccinations. Many countries still require vaccination against smallpox, cholera, and yellow fever as a condition of entry, and the PHS continues to recommend vaccinations for persons going to areas where specific diseases are prevalent. In addition, the PHS may impose new requirements as conditions change.

238

According to the PHS Center for Disease Control in Atlanta, American travelers should, for their own protection, obtain vaccination against some diseases irrespective of what particular countries demand.

The PHS also urges immunization against tetanus and diphtheria for all travelers and vaccination against diseases such as polio, typhus, hepatitis, and plague depending on what countries you plan to visit and expected living accommodations. Travel to remote, rural areas of some countries, for example, may make you a more likely candidate for vaccination than if you plan to stay in more highly developed areas usually frequented by tourists.

Before traveling abroad, the PHS suggests, check with your local health department to determine which vaccinations are required or recommended. A spokesman for the Center of Disease Control emphasizes that requirements imposed by either the U.S. Government or foreign governments can change at any time, depending on disease outbreaks.

"We can be lenient today," he notes, "but it may well be we can't be lenient tomorrow."

Pet-Travel Hazards

AIRLINES are forever telling air travelers how well they'll fly in the friendly skies, on the wings of man, or with Cheryl. But how do these accommodating folks treat your dogs, cats, and other pets when they're along for the ride, down among the suitcases? Perhaps not very well, say some critics.

Consumer Reports, published by Consumers Union, says animals have suffocated in the cargo compartments of some planes, whose on-ground temperatures may reach 130 degrees. They say also that contrary to the impression many pet owners have that animals traveling in these compartments enjoy conditions similar to those in the passenger cabin, many luggage pits have no air circulating in them. Such pits are sealed to prevent the spread of fire, but the safety precaution also limits the animals' oxygen to what is sealed in.

An article in Air Line Pilot, the magazine of the Air Line Pilots Association, says, "Death, injury, or loss of live animals and birds has apparently reached a point where the nation's humane societies consider it a major issue in their crusade for better treatment of all living creatures."

How bad is the problem? Consumer Reports says "it's impossible to determine the exact risks of shipping a pet by air." A spokesman for the Air Transport Association of American, the scheduled airlines' trade association, estimates about 200,000 dogs and cats are moved by air each year and says association records show only

240

about 300 claims—a fraction of one per cent—are made yearly against carriers for dead or injured animals. Association records do not reflect accidents for which no claims are made.

The airlines say they have detailed guidelines to assure animal safety. A spokesman for American Airlines says that because there is no air flow in many luggage compartments, they have a "minimum-animal rule," which guarantees they won't transport more animals than the oxygen supply allows for. "We will turn away freight to give animals space," he says.

A United Air Lines employe says that after the Consumer Reports article appeared she checked the conditions for animal travel in United's planes. "We do have a pit in each craft that is properly air conditioned or heated," she says.

But reassuring statistics and guidelines apparently didn't satisfy a man whose Irish wolfhound arrived dead on a flight from Dallas to Miami. He went after the offending 727 with an ax, chopped holes in its belly, and threw paint on it. Veterinarians performing autopsies on animals that arrive dead after flights usually attribute death to suffocation, and both airlines and pet owners can be blamed for the deaths of these animals.

Most deaths seem to occur on the ground, and most often during hot summer months when there are delays before take-off or unloading and luggage compartments overheat. The airlines insist this can't happen on newer planes whose luggage holds receive circulating air from the passenger cabins. But the holds on older aircraft are indeed sealed to prevent fire, and airline spokesmen admit that until the craft is in flight on a hot day, on-ground temperatures in the hold can get quite high.

Sometimes unfeeling or ignorant pet owners cause

problems for their animals by shipping them in poorly made, poorly ventilated crates. Humane societies say they have seen dogs and cats moved in cardboard boxes with a few air holes punched in the sides, in slatted fruit crates, and in poorly designed homemade kennels. Animals not given enough room for stretching have slashed themselves badly on protruding nails, or cut their mouths chewing through their wire cells.

Further aggravating the problem is the fact that airlines and cargo handlers on the ground are not obligated to care for animals beyond complying with loading guidelines and handling crates carefully. During delays they don't have to feed, water, or exercise the animals; if an animal looks sick, it's not their problem.

The American Society for the Prevention of Cruelty to Animals has established an Animalport at Kennedy International Airport in New York City. At the pet owner's expense, Animal port cares for animals 24 hours a day, has a veterinarian on call, provides ambulance service for sick animals. There are animal-care centers at other airports, but they are rare and they are less elaborate than Animalport.

Can anything be done to improve the lot of traveling animals? Consumers Union urged the Civil Aeronautics Board (CAB) to establish compartment standards for animals, including permissible ranges for temperature, pressurization, oxygen, and noise levels.

A CAB official said, however, that it is unlikely the board would initiate any action on its own. The board isn't sure it has statutory authority to set standards for transporting animals, and airlines almost surely would challenge any attempt to do so. The official said that if humane societies felt strongly about animal treatment aboard aircraft, they should make a formal complaint to the CAB, which then would be obligated to investigate the matter.

Republican Sen. Lowell P. Weicker of Connecticut is pushing for a law that would direct the Secretary of Transportation to set regulations assuring humane treatment for animals shipped by air. Weicker has offered his bill as an amendment to the Animal Welfare Act of 1970.

There are a number of precautions a pet owner can take to make an animal's trip safer and more comfortable:

● A good kennel is the best thing you can provide your pet, and a good kennel is not just a box with holes in it. A good kennel must be sturdy to prevent escape, must have proper ventilation, must give the animal room to move, must have a floor able to retain wastes, and ought to have some deodorized bedding it it. If you can't build a proper kennel, buy one from a pet store, or check with the airline; some rent or sell kennels.

● Give the airline as much notice as possible. A person arriving unannounced at an airport is generally well-treated; the same may not be true for animals.

● Avoid shipping your pet in midday during the summer. Some animals are more sensitive to hot weather than others, and the temperatures around and in aircraft during the summer can get very hot. In hot weather the airlines suggest shipping pets in the evening.

You might also have a veterinarian check your pet before traveling. Air travel can be traumatic for a pet, and a vet can provide tranquilizers if necessary. Some animals have gone berserk at the roar of jet engines and broken out of their cages. A sick animal shouldn't travel at all.

How to Car Pool

A blue station wagon quietly approached a house, still shrouded in darkness. A lamp silhouetted the figure of a man hovering near a house window. He made it to the door even before the signal, a short blast of the horn. He strode resolutely toward the car.

Ed Hokanson wasted no time because he knows the rule: no waiting. If you're not ready the others will go without you. He is a member of a car pool that's been a long-standing success; car-pool failures are more the norm.

Ed agrees with his fellow riders that unbendable rules, such as no waiting, help avoid possible conflicts and inconveniences that worry many a would-be car pooler.

Gas shortages have prompted people who once would have shunned a shared ride to try it. Others have signed up with one of the proliferating corporate and community computer efforts to pool employes.

What these novices need, say these veterans from the suburb of Prairie Village, Kan., is a clear understanding of what they expect of each other and at least a moderate amount of consideration.

Some of their rules: All the riders must be picked up no later than 7:45 a.m. to assure arrival by about 8:10 a.m. in downtown Kansas City, Mo. The homeward-bound trip leaves promptly at 5:25 p.m. Each member must drive on his designed weekday, with membership kept at five to avoid scheduling problems. A vacationing or sick member must arrange for a stand-in and make up the driving

244

chores on return. No cars too small for five with accompanying briefcases may be used.

There are accommodations: A car with snow tires in place likely will be used, regardless of schedule, if there's an early snow.

The Prairie Village pool dates back to 1962, though charter member Walt Wolfert, 55, has been riding to work in car pools since 1953. Don Dorn, 37, joined Wolfert's group in 1963, while Dave Nordquist, 35, Hokanson, 32, and Rose Mary Teaford, 52, replaced dropouts since 1970.

All work at Hallmark Cards, Inc., which promotes car pools by providing a full-time co-ordinator, computer time to match employes, and close-in parking lots for car poolers only. The Prairie Village group predates the company's emphasis on car pooling, but another Hallmark pool put together with corporate help works just as smoothly because of similar rules.

Once again, the main one is "no waiting."

Dorothy Bohanon, 37, does all the driving for five other women who also live in western Kansas City, Kan. "That keeps things routine. I never walked in anywhere late in my life," she says.

"You can set a clock by her," agrees Alice Moore, 49, who has been sharing rides since World War II.

Pooling is so much a part of some riders' lives that it's more than cheap transportation. The Prairie Village pool is a place to exchange tips on investments, a forum for Friday-afternoon puns. And the ride in Dorothy's car is the equivalent of a neighborly chat for women going off to work instead of next door for coffee.

"I would prefer to be in it than to drive alone because I enjoy visiting with the people," says Don, adding that he would miss the group if he had to quit. Ed says the pool saves him $6 a week and spares his nose and ears from a bus-stop chill. Dave is happy because his can remain a one-car family. Rose Mary appreciates relief from "battling traffic, the cost of gas, and the general strain of driving by yourself."

Walt, a man of few words, explains that he can't compare the car pool with other types of commuting because pooling is the only way he's known.

Dorothy is an outgoing secretary who admits she wants to keep the conversation going on rides both to and from. That's fine for Linda Dalton, 27, who found her pool through Hallmark's computer shortly after she began work there. "It wakes you up when you get in and start talking," she says. "The ride to work seemed twice as far when I drove in all by myself." Because of the camaraderie, La Donna Newport, 26, says she would prefer to ride in the pool "even if the bus came right to my door and I could afford it."

Conversation in both pools seems to be a reflection of the personal interests of the riders. On a recent trip with Dorothy's group, for example, the women wished rider Marge Hale a happy 24th birthday, then talked about baking cakes, a church contata, a TV show, and what kind of new car the Bohanons should buy.

The Prairie Village group spent a similar ride discussing a son's ski trip, a junior-high drug raid, the price of silver, and the merits of collecting coins, antiques, and paintings. "My bother finished a painting last night and has already sold it to a girl in his apartment building," Ed contributed. "Paint by numbers?" quipped Dave. "Look like he spilled an egg on it?" quipped Walt.

If a rider doesn't feel up to either quipping or reviewing a book, the Prairie Village riders say there's no stigma for silence on a difficult morning or after a hard day at work. "And we don't talk about politics and religion," Rose Mary adds.

Many of the riders contend their car pools are therapeutic. "There's a joy in being able to sound off about things at work," says Don. La Donna has a similar view: "If I'm mad about something that happens at the office, I can get several opinions from people who know the situation. Husbands just don't understand."

La Donna also believes riding in the pool makes the whole corporation seem less impersonal to her because she hears about people and activities in other departments.

For Hallmark, car-pooling benefits generally are perceived as more concrete. Often it's a matter of avoiding the cost of an expensive parking lot or new access road. Relief of congestion and the resulting tardiness and projection of a positive leadership image were also noted.

The energy crunch and the rising cost of gasoline have given impetus to the car-pool movement for companies and riders alike. When riders are asked to cite benefits, economics prevail. Hallmark co-ordinator Tom Williams says employes are signing up who say they weren't even remotely interested when matching began.

It's not computer dating: The company matches employes by location and work shift only. "It's certainly difficult if some riders don't mind being late and others practically have heart failure over the prospect," he observes. In that situation, it's probably best to try for a rematch.

Of course some people simply find conforming to rules and time schedules a great burden. Take Marge Hale, who admits she's part of a three-alarm-clock family. One fall morning driver Dorothy pulled up in front of a still-dark house, then detoured the pool to a nearby food store to call and wake up Marge. "I took my own car later,"

Marge recalls, "but the experience upset me. I felt uptight about it with the others."

Marge also confesses difficulty with the early-morning socializing. "I have a 4-year-old daughter, so driving to work used to be my only quiet time. I miss it," she says.

One Hallmark employe, who begged anonymity, belongs to another pool that she declares a daily disaster. The four members have failed to work out a firm schedule. Instead one person calls everyone else each morning to bicker over who takes the car. The disgruntled secretary says she recently had to drive three days in one work week. "We wait at night as late as 6:20 because one guy just won't leave anybody. He goes in the building and looks. And of course nobody is ever on time in the morning. Still, I'd rather be late than spend money on gas!"

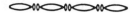

LONDON-BOUND visitors planning an extensive stay will find a broad variety of useful information in *The Book of London* (Links Books, 33 W. 60th St., New York City 10023; 315 pages; $2.95 in paperback). The book, for example, suggests ways for hiring tradesmen, reviews credit practices in London stores, tells how to obtain psychiatric care, and catalogs some dating services.